Integrating the ESL Standards Into Classroom Practice:
Grades 3-5

Katharine Davies Samway, Editor

WRITERS

Sue DeFabbia

Jim Hughes

Linda New Levine

Carlyn Syvanen

Dorothy Taylor

Suzanne Irujo, Series Editor

Teachers of English to Speakers of Other Languages, Inc.

Typeset in Optima with Dolphin display
by Capitol Communications Systems, Inc., Crofton, Maryland USA
and printed by Pantagraph Printing, Bloomington, Illinois USA

Teachers of English to Speakers of Other Languages, Inc.
700 South Washington Street, Suite 200
Alexandria, Virginia 22314 USA
Tel. 703-836-0774 • Fax 703-836-7864 • E-mail tesol@tesol.org • http://www.tesol.org/

Director of Communications and Marketing: Helen Kornblum
Managing Editor: Marilyn Kupetz
Copy Editors: Ellen Garshick and Christa Watters
Cover Design: Charles Akins and Ann Kammerer

ISBN 0-939791-85-4
Library of Congress Catalogue No. 00 130569

Contents

Acknowledgments

Writing this volume has been a powerful learning experience for us all. It has been a particular pleasure to have learned from and with each other.

The volume has been enhanced in untold ways by the always thoughtful, supportive, ingenious, and speedy support provided to us by Suzanne Irujo (series editor) and Marilyn Kupetz (managing editor). They have been models of professionalism throughout, and we are very grateful for all they have done to help us bring this volume to publication.

The volume could not have come about without the input of the editors of the other volumes in this series, Barbara Agor, Suzanne Irujo, and Betty Ansin Smallwood, along with the chair of TESOL's Publications Committee, Kathleen Graves. Those long-distance phone calls and e-mail messages were stimulating and helped us develop our own vision.

We are grateful to our family members, who have supported us as we have completed this volume, even in the midst of moving, traveling, coping with family illness, and starting new and demanding jobs.

We have saved our final thanks for the students with whom we worked, and whose voices, thoughts, intelligence, and creativity are in these pages. Through them, we have learned to be better teachers.

Series Editor's Preface

When I first saw a copy of *ESL Standards for Pre-K–12 Students* (TESOL, 1997), I thought, "These are very well done, but how are teachers going to use them?" Working with teachers since then, I've heard them echo those thoughts: "I really like these standards, but I'm not sure how to use them in my classroom."

The four volumes in the series *Integrating the ESL Standards Into Classroom Practice* are designed to help teachers use the standards. The series covers four sets of grade levels: pre-K–2, 3–5, 6–8, and 9–12. Each volume contains six units, some designed with a particular grade level or proficiency level in mind, others designed to span grade and proficiency levels. There are units for very specific contexts and units that are more general. All the units are adaptable for other levels and contexts and include suggestions for doing that.

These units were taught and written by real teachers, each of whom approaches the implementation of the ESL standards in the classroom in a different way. As I worked on editing the four volumes, I was struck by the wide variety of ways in which teachers who work with standards use them to inform their teaching. In describing what skills must be mastered by ESOL students in public schools, the standards become planning tools, observational aids, assessment guides, and ways of understanding language development.

These units also exemplify the strategies that Lachat (1999) recommends for teachers implementing standards-based instruction:

- Organize learning around what students need to know and be able to do
- Enrich their teaching by cultivating students' higher order thinking processes
- Guide student inquiry by posing real-life tasks that require reasoning and problem-solving
- Emphasize holistic concepts rather than fragmented units of information
- Provide a variety of opportunities for students to explore and confront concepts and situations over time
- Use multiple sources of information rather than a single text
- Work in interdisciplinary teams
- Use multiple forms of assessment to gather concrete evidence of student proficiencies (p. 13)

The teachers who prepared these units did so to demonstrate what they did when they taught the units, not to tell others what should be done. The units were designed to serve several purposes. We wanted them to be complete, finished products, usable as they are in other classrooms, so we made them as explicit as we could. We wanted them to be adaptable for use in other situations and contexts, so we included suggestions for doing that. We wanted them to serve as possible models for teachers who want to develop their own standards-based units, so we provided explanations for why we did things as we did.

These volumes expand upon and complement the work contained in previous TESOL standards publications. We have used appropriate descriptors and sample progress indicators as they appear for each standard in *ESL Standards for Pre-K–12 Students* (TESOL, 1997), although we have also created some new progress indicators when appropriate. We have tried to incorporate the assessment process outlined in *Managing the Assessment Process: A Framework for Measuring Student Attainment of the ESL Standards* (TESOL, 1998). Many of the checklists and rubrics used in the assessment sections are adaptations of those found in *Scenarios for ESL Standards-Based Assessment* (TESOL, in press).

A few technical notes:

- In keeping with the terminology used in *ESL Standards* (TESOL, 1997), we use *ESL* (English as a second language) to refer to the standards, the field, and our classes. We use *ESOL* (English to speakers of other languages) to refer to the learners themselves.

- In order to avoid having to repeat detailed procedures for teaching techniques that appear in several units in a volume, we have included a glossary of techniques. Because of this, there is no glossary of terms, but definitions of standards-related terms are available in *ESL Standards* (TESOL, 1997) and *Scenarios* (TESOL, in press).

- All resources and references for each unit are listed at the end of the unit. Writers annotated the resources where they felt it would be helpful to readers.

Our hope in producing these volumes is that teachers will be able to use these units in their own classes and that they will also gain insights into incorporating the ESL standards into other units they may develop. We want them to be able to say, after reading one or several units, "Now I know what to do with the ESL standards in my classroom."

Suzanne Irujo, Series Editor

REFERENCES

Lachat, M. A. (1999). *Standards, equity and cultural diversity.* Providence, RI: Northeast and Islands Regional Educational Laboratory at Brown University (LAB).

TESOL. (1997). *ESL standards for pre-K–12 students.* Alexandria, VA: Author.

TESOL. (1998). *Managing the assessment process: A framework for measuring student attainment of the ESL standards* (TESOL Professional Paper No. 5). Alexandria, VA: Author.

TESOL. (in press). *Scenarios for ESL standards-based assessment.* Alexandria, VA: Author.

Introduction

Over the many months that it took us to write this book, I would often read drafts in the middle of the night, when all I could hear was the sound of sleeping bodies shifting in their beds, the occasional blare of a freight train passing through the city center, or the alarming shrieks of neighborhood cats protecting their territory. Even when reading early drafts, when ideas were barely formed, I would rejoice at the range of meaningful learning events that these teachers offered their students, the ways in which they followed the lead of their students, both in terms of content and language teaching. "These are observant, thoughtful teachers who are constantly rethinking their practice," I would think.

I was curious to learn more about how standards influenced their lives as teachers and the learning of their students. My curiosity was further sparked by the often shrill and discordant attention paid to standards and high-stakes testing by politicians and the media. Today, standards are often touted as a panacea for the perceived ills in education. But as a teacher, I know that standards in and of themselves will not remedy those ills, whether real or imagined. Some teachers may use standards as the major factor in instructional decision making, without paying any attention to the accomplishments and needs of students. In this case, the standards may be covered, but will children have learned much? In contrast, a teacher can use the standards as a guide, a resource to refer to when making instructional decisions, to ensure that ESOL students are enabled to develop a full range of academic and social language as well as sociocultural knowledge, and to do so in a way that is appropriate for their level of learning, strengths, and needs.

I know that there is very little point in teaching concepts, skills, or content that students already have control of and understand. Similarly, there is no point in teaching concepts, skills, or content far beyond the grasp of learners at that moment. Ongoing assessment in natural learning contexts tells me what learners are able to do and understand and what they seem ready to assimilate, and it is this latter information that helps me decide what to teach. Then I need to figure out how I am going to teach it, how I will group students for instruction, and how I will organize the day and instruction for optimal teaching and learning.

I was not sure how standards fit into this philosophical stance, but working on this volume has helped me see how they can aid in identifying potential gaps. Through working with a group of thoughtful and well-informed educators, I understand the important role that standards can play in enhancing the education of ESOL students. As each of the writers points out, standards act as a reminder—a very important reminder—of the range of issues to consider when making instructional decisions. The standards remind us that ESOL students may lack some very important skills, both in academic and in interpersonal situations. The standards do not have to limit us, as I once feared. They do not have to dictate to us, as I once assumed. They can remind us and, in the process, keep us on our toes.

You will find slightly different pedagogical stances and teaching styles in this volume. I did not seek conformity among writers, recognizing that we are all individuals, with different professional experiences and preparation, and different students. I hope that you recognize yourself to some extent in these pages, and that you will be encouraged to further explore the role of standards in your teaching and the best, most meaningful way of enhancing your students' learning and success in and with English.

Although the six units reflect very different teachers, I think that you will find some common elements. First, these teachers often followed the lead of their students. Although they planned instruction carefully, as they listened and observed, they often found that they needed to move away from the prepared lesson plan and teach the students other content, skills, and strategies. Sometimes they would follow the suggestions and requests of students to study unanticipated content. Second, these teachers often had to rethink their practice after realizing that an activity was not successful. I hope that you will find their honesty realistic and refreshing. Also, I hope that you will see how these temporary blocks in their paths did not stop the teachers; instead, they learned from and integrated the knowledge they gained from the experience, moved on, and provided students with an even better learning experience.

Two of the units are actually segments from much longer units. Jim Hughes' "Writing for Each Other" (Unit 2) occurred in the first 4 weeks of school and was part of a year-long project that focused on learning about, respecting, and integrating the home culture into school learning. Carlyn Syvanen's "Recycling" (Unit 6) is a 6-week component in a year-round project undertaken by an advanced-level ESL class. Students in this class did more than simply learn about recycling; they were responsible for the school's recycling program.

Some of the units arose out of the confusion, tedium, and exhaustion that often accompany the end of the school year or particularly difficult classes. Sue DeFabbia met with her group of challenging third- and fourth-grade ESOL students at the end of the school day. Her students learned a lot through preparing for and creating a board game that reflected their learning about the Underground Railroad (Unit 4); they took this game around the school to play with other classes. Linda New Levine introduced her third-grade students to their unit about Central America and the rain forest, "The Most Beautiful Place in the World" (Unit 5), as a means to bolster her Latino students' self-esteem and help them learn to interact more effectively with each other. Syvanen's "Native Americans, Then and Now" (Unit 1) was taught in May, after she and her students had "survived April, the month of testing . . . definitely the low point of the year." The unit emerged out of an independent reading program that she had instituted to counter all the interruptions and disruptions caused by the testing, and was an answer to lagging student interest.

On occasion, the units were closely tied to district or state content requirements, but in all cases, the teachers went beyond these requirements to ensure that the units were tailored to their ESOL students' needs. For example, Dorothy Taylor's "Facing Hardship: Jamestown and Colonial Life" (Unit 3) was grounded in the need for her students to take a state history test; it was also a response to students' interest in this era, an interest that grew out of a field trip with their mainstream classes. "The Underground

Railroad" was an integral part of the district's history curriculum (Rochester was an important stop on the Underground Railroad) and fell during Black History Month.

All but one of the unit writers is a pullout ESL teacher. The classes they wrote about ranged in size from 6 to 20 students. Syvanen implemented "Native Americans, Then and Now" with 16 students in a 2-hour block of reading/math time when all children in the grade were divided among all teachers, both mainstream and specialists, for appropriate instruction. DeFabbia is an itinerant ESL teacher who divides her time between an elementary school and a middle school. Taylor and Levine work in elementary schools. Hughes is the sole self-contained, mainstream teacher in this volume; he worked with 20 students. Like Syvanen and DeFabbia, Hughes works in an urban, multiethnic, multilingual school. Taylor works in a large suburban school district, and Levine works in a small suburban district.

We did the major part of our work in writing this volume in the summer. Long before the summer arrived, however, I had contacted scores of colleagues (teachers and teacher educators around the country and in the TESOL community) for names of potential writers, good teachers who might be interested in writing a unit and able to do so in the summer. I value enormously, and am very grateful to have had, the opportunity to work closely with this group of writer-teachers. They have taught me a lot about teaching ESOL children, through their writing, through our many e-mail communications, and through the long phone calls when we clarified things. I hope that your thinking and practice will be similarly enriched.

Katharine Davies Samway, Editor

UNIT 1
Native Americans, Then and Now

CARLYN SYVANEN

Introduction

> *My students and I had just survived April, the month of testing. We were all feeling frustrated and tired of school. Our regular program had been disrupted for the full month to schedule the tests in reading, math, science, and social studies. It was definitely the low point of the year. To keep some real reading going on during the testing period, I was having students read independently. The students chose their own books, read them, met with me for brief conferences, and filled out a reading response sheet for each book read. Interest was lagging. They were spending more time choosing books, visiting with neighbors, or just staring into space, than reading.*

I have found that if I am spending more of my time than usual redirecting students, it is time for me to look at what needs to be changed. I had begun reading O'Dell and Hall's (1992) *Thunder Rolling in the Mountains* to the students. In my observations of read-alouds in the regular education classes, I had noticed that the ESOL students were not expected to listen to or follow the story. As a result, my fourth- and fifth-grade students had developed very poor listening skills during read-aloud time. At the beginning of the year, my students were unable to retell what I had just read to them. To encourage the students to become more active listeners, my read-alouds consisted of very short readings, not more than 10 minutes and usually less. After the read-aloud, tables of four

---

Context

Grade levels: Fourth and fifth grade

English proficiency level: Intermediate

Native languages of students: Cambodian, Haitian Creole, Russian, Somali, Spanish, Tongan

Focus of instruction: Reading/social studies

Type of class: Literacy/math block

Length of unit: 6 weeks

---

students earned points by retelling something that they remembered from the reading. They needed to listen to what others were saying because they were not allowed to repeat what someone else had already said. During these follow-up discussions, I noticed that my students were more interested than usual in the book. Also, they asked questions that helped them understand events in the book that were not clear to them. (All students' names are pseudonyms except for Anna and Bumi, which are used with permission.)

Filsan:	Did she really shoot the soldier?
Manuel:	Yeah. He burnt a house?
Teacher:	In the book it says [rereading part of the paragraph], ". . . wild thoughts flashed through my mind. I saw myself riding into the soldiers' camp with a torch, setting fire to their tents. I saw myself take aim with my rifle and shoot a soldier from his horse" (O'Dell & Hall, 1992, p. 17).
Uilou:	Oh, she imagination.

My students were 15 fourth- and fifth-grade intermediate-level ESOL students. Some students had been in U.S. schools since kindergarten but were reading at least 2 years below grade level. Others had arrived in the United States 2 years before and were literate in their first languages. My students were from Cambodia, Haiti, Liberia, Mexico, Panama, Russia, Somalia, and Tonga. We met for a 2-hour period each day, with 1 hour dedicated to reading and the other to math. During this 6-week period, our reading time usually ran 15 or 20 minutes longer than the allotted hour. This extra time on reading had been offset earlier in the year when we spent more than an hour on math in preparation for the statewide fifth-grade math problem-solving exam.

I met with this group of students for a 2-hour block each day because 2 years earlier the school staff had decided to adopt a 2-hour prime-time schedule in the morning. During this time, all teachers (ESOL, Chapter 1, and classroom) had a group of students for reading and math, and there were no pullouts. As a consequence, Chapter 1 and ESOL teachers had the advantage of working with students for a longer period of time. Classroom teachers had smaller groups to work with and were not driven to distraction by the constant coming and going of pullout groups. One of the ESOL teachers met with beginners while the remaining three ESOL teachers met with intermediate-level groups. We met with the more advanced students in 30- to 40-minute pullout sessions at other times. Each ESOL teacher met with 40–50 students during the course of the week.

Unit Overview

My students' interest in *Thunder Rolling in the Mountains* (O'Dell & Hall, 1992) showed me the way to reengage their interest in the class. I decided that we would finish out the year with a study of Native Americans. As I sat down to plan, I needed to take several factors into consideration. For example, as this was their reading instruction time, I would need to find multiple copies of several books for **reading circles**. Also, as I wanted the students to gather information from a number of sources, I would need to find nonfiction books for the reading circles as well as a wide selection of library books and films from the school district's audiovisual library.

My goal for this unit was for the students to learn that several different native cultures had existed throughout North America and that Native Americans of today live

Unit Overview: Native Americans, Then and Now

Introductory Activity
• K-W-L chart

Read-Aloud Activity
• *Thunder Rolling in the Mountains*

Reading Circle Activities
• Book choice
• Sample activities
  — *Children of the Wind and Water*
  — *A Mare for Young Wolf*
  — *Young Wolf's First Hunt*
  — Vocabulary and grammar teaching
  — Computer work
  — Assessment and record keeping

Other Activities
• Film
• Moccasin making
• Modern Native Americans
• Culminating activity

very differently from the way they lived before contact with Europeans. I also wanted them to be able to use information from various sources to understand that knowledge about Native Americans is multifaceted, not simplistic.

The unit included several different sources of information and a variety of teaching methods. I directed read-alouds and films to the whole group, and planned whole-group, partner, and individual activities around them. The books read during reading circle led to small-group and individual activities. The collection of library books in the room was for partner and individual activities.

The unit overview shown above shows the sequence of activities. There were 5 weeks of read-alouds, which took place first thing on Monday through Thursday mornings and lasted 10–15 minutes. I then met with either two or three reading circles each day. On days when we had additional activities or films, I was able to meet with two reading circles.

Standards

As I was planning the unit, I reviewed *ESL Standards for Pre-K–12 Students* (TESOL, 1997), which made me aware of some of the gaps in my program that year. Because of a scheduling decision, our literacy block had become 1 hour of reading and 1 hour of math; writing was covered in the homeroom classrooms. As a result, I felt I had not adequately addressed Goal 1 (To use English to communicate in social settings) and Goal 3 (To use English in socially and culturally appropriate ways) to the extent I had in previous years. I placed a note in my planning file to remind me not to fall short in subsequent years.

Introductory Activity

This 6-week unit included long-term activities, such as read-alouds and daily reading circles, and shorter term activities, such as generating a **K-W-L chart** and viewing a film. The "Six-Week Schedule" shown on page 5 more clearly establishes the sequence of activities.

K-W-L Chart

I knew that the students had some knowledge of Native Americans from our read-aloud of *Thunder Rolling in the Mountains* (O'Dell & Hall, 1992), which had begun before this unit formally started and lasted into its fifth week. I knew that they had studied aspects of Native American life and history in their third-grade classes or as part of their study of Oregon history in fourth grade and U.S. history in fifth grade. Also, earlier in the year, most of the students had read either *Young Wolf's First Hunt* (Shefelman, 1995) or *The True Story of Pocahontas* (Penner, 1994) in their reading circles. I expected that they would contribute quite a bit of information to the K-W-L chart that I used to introduce the unit.

Goal 2, Standard 2   To use English to achieve academically in all content areas: Students will use English to obtain, process, construct, and provide subject matter information in spoken and written form.

Descriptors

- listening to, speaking, reading, and writing about subject matter information
- gathering information orally and in writing
- selecting, connecting, and explaining information
- formulating and asking questions

Progress Indicators

- synthesize, analyze, and evaluate information
- locate information appropriate to an assignment in text or reference materials

---

PROCEDURE

- On the third day of the unit, I explained that we were going to embark on a study of Native Americans. I mentioned that we were reading a book about the Nez Perce and that some of us had read *Young Wolf's First Hunt* or *The True Story of Pocahontas* in our reading circles earlier in the year. I said that

Six-Week Schedule

	Monday	Tuesday	Wednesday	Thursday	Friday
Week 1					
9:05–9:20	Chapter 4	*Teacher read-aloud, map updates*			
		Chapter 5	Chapter 6	Chapter 7	
9:20–10:20	Book choice activity	3 reading circles	2 reading circles K-W-L	3 reading circles	2 reading circles Find answers in library books
Week 2					
9:05–9:20	Chapter 8	*Teacher read-aloud; map updates; retellings*			
		Chapter 9	Chapter 10	Chapter 11	
9:20–10:20	3 reading circles	2 reading circles Film: *Had You Lived Then*	2 reading circles Venn diagram	3 reading circles	2 reading circles Making moccasins
Week 3					
9:05–9:20	Chapter 12	*Teacher read-aloud, map updates, retellings*			
		Chapter 13	Chapter 14	Chapter 15	
9:20–10:20			3 reading circles	2 reading circles Film: *I Will Fight No More*, Part 1	2 reading circles Film: *I Will Fight No More*, Part 2
Week 4					
9:05–9:20	Chapter 16	*Teacher read-aloud; map updates; retellings*			
		Chapter 17	Chapter 18	Chapter 19	
9:20–10:20	3 reading circles	3 reading circles	3 reading circles	2 reading circles Film: *I Will Fight No More*, Part 3	2 reading circles Film: *I Will Fight No More*, Part 4
Week 5					
9:05–9:20	Chapter 20	*Teacher read-aloud, map updates, retellings*			
		Chapter 21	Chapter 22	Chapter 23	
9:20–10:20	2 reading circles Film: *Indian Summer*	2 reading circles Teacher reads *Buffalo Days*; discussion	2 reading circles	3 reading circles	2 reading circles Make tipis
Week 6					
9:05–9:45	2 reading circles	2 reading circles	2 reading circles	2 reading circles	Reports
9:45–10:15		Culminating projects			Self-evaluation

we would start out by listing everything that we knew about Native Americans.

- As the students made contributions, I wrote them on an overhead transparency. The list of information that the students generated about Native Americans was disappointingly short and was limited to information that they had gained in our class; they did not refer to other sources of knowledge. I wondered later if the students' contributions were limited because they did not know more or if they thought I was asking only for what they had learned in class.

K-W-Ls can be useful in activating prior knowledge; however, students may perceive them as a test of what I have taught them. In future K-W-L activities, I will ask questions that encourage students to draw on a wider knowledge base—for example, questions more directly related to units of study in their other classes, such as, "When you read about the Oregon Trail, what did you learn about Native Americans?" or "Did you study about Native Americans in third grade? What do you remember about that?"

- I later transferred the lists of what the students knew and wanted to know from the overhead projector to chart paper so that we could refer back to them throughout the unit, adding questions and answering those we could, as the students found new information. The first day's K-W-L chart is shown below.

- After we had read through our list of questions again, I briefly introduced a collection of books about Native Americans that I had gathered from the local library. Originally, I had wanted the class to use the school library to research their questions, but in a preliminary search, I found that our library had very few books on the topic.

K-W-L Chart

Native Americans

What We Know	What We Want to Know	What We Learned
• They hunted different ways from each other. • They lived in tipis. • They made canoes out of hollow logs. • They traded. • They used bows and arrows. • They used buffalo horns to make stuff	• How did they make tents? • What did they use for bathrooms? • How can you make things out of rock? • How did they get clean? • How did they know sign language? • Did all Native Americans live in tipis? • Did the children go to school? • Did they learn the ABCs?	

- I asked the students to browse through the books in order to find answers to their questions.

- The books remained in the classroom, and the students returned to them from time to time during the 6-week cycle.

Read-Aloud Activity

Thunder Rolling in the Mountains

For the read-aloud, I had chosen *Thunder Rolling in the Mountains* (O'Dell & Hall, 1992). From the beginning of the school year, I had been choosing books of increasing length and complexity, and I felt the class was now ready for a book of this length and difficulty. The book also fit into my goal of reading about people from a variety of ethnic groups. Chief Joseph is a local hero whom the students had encountered in their studies of Oregon history, and the story starts in eastern Oregon. Four days a week, I read a chapter of the book as the students listened; we finished the book in the fifth week of this unit. From the discussion following each session, it was clear that the students had very little background knowledge of this historical period or of Native American life. I realized that to understand the book they were listening to, my students would need more visuals.

The book browsing activity was not as successful as it often is. In retrospect, I realized that because we had gotten a late start that morning, I had rushed my explanation of the task, and the students were not clear about what to do. After the introduction to the activity, I began working with reading circles and was not available to clarify any misunderstandings. From this session, I learned, again, how important it is to prepare carefully and offer clear directions.

Goal 2, Standard 1 **To use English to achieve academically in all content areas: Students will use English to interact in the classroom.**

Descriptors

- following oral and written directions, implicit and explicit
- requesting and providing clarification
- participating in full-class, group, and pair discussions
- asking and answering questions

Progress Indicators

- use polite forms to negotiate and reach consensus
- take turns when speaking in a group
- modify a statement made by a peer

PROCEDURE

To help my students develop better listening skills, I read for no more than 10 minutes at a time. After I finished reading, I gave each table of about four students 1 point for orally sharing with the class information they had gained from the chapter. To encourage them to listen to each other, students got points only for information that no one else had mentioned. My questions were usually general, such as "What happened to-day?" But when I felt a key piece of information had been missed, I asked more focused questions. On Monday mornings, after 3 days away from the story, I asked for volunteers to bring us up-to-date.

- I copied the map of the route of the Nez Perce from the front of the book, enlarged it, and pinned it up above the U.S. map on the bulletin board so the students could see the location of the route. Each day, after we had discussed the events in that day's reading, we would decide what was the most important idea of the day, write it on a sticky note, and put it in the appropriate place on the map. We numbered the sticky notes so that we could use them later to retell the story.

There were a few students who rarely answered questions about the story but did a good job of bringing us up-to-date. I think that these students were not confident about their ability to understand the language of the book but benefited from their peers' retelling.

- About halfway through the unit, we watched a feature-length film, *I Will Fight No More Forever* (Wolper Productions, 1975), which covered the same time period as the book. It came in four 20-minute segments, and I showed it in four sessions spread over 2 weeks. It was a Hollywood-made film but included dramatizations of some of the incidents that are described in the book. The film stimulated very animated discussions, and the students' comments showed that they were making connections between the film and the book, as the excerpts from conversations show. Students commented while watching the film:

Miguel: [as soon as he saw the soldiers' uniforms in the movie] Oh, that is why they call them Blue Coats.
Uilou: Why the old woman go in the woods?
Jesse: Yesterday in the book it say old people get tired and go away and die.
Uilou: Ahhh.
Filsan: Teacher, why do the White people want to kill the Indians?

Students commented during discussions of the book:

Stephanie: The girl [Sound of Running Feet, Chief Joseph's 14-year-old daughter, who is featured in the book] isn't in the movie. I like this story better.
Justin: Chief Joseph's wife is dead, but not in the movie.

- As I previewed each chapter, I pulled pictures from my picture file or collection of books on Native Americans so that I could illustrate for the students terms in the story that they might not understand, such as *buffalo horn ladles* and *horse drawn travois*.

Reading Circle Activities

The reading circles lasted for the entire unit. I selected three books so that we would have three groups of five for our reading circles. I kept the groups small (no more than six students) so that I could more easily keep track of students' reading strategies and note places where comprehension broke down. Also, one of the workstations during reading circles was computer work, and we had six computers in the room.

In the course of our reading circle each morning, students typically rotated through three activities. I tried to meet with each of the three book groups daily, and when students were not meeting with me, they continued reading, wrote responses to book-based prompts that I gave them in their reading logs, and worked on the computer. When we had a whole-group activity, such as a film, students usually rotated through just two activities. The sample reading circle schedule below illustrates this rotation.

In the hour dedicated to reading, I met with three groups a day or, on those days when we had a whole group project, I met with two groups. So that the students and I could keep track of where we needed to be, I used a system of colored cards on a

---

Sample Reading Circle Schedule

	Read With Teacher	Independent Work	Computer Work
9:20	*Young Wolf's First Hunt:* Discuss pp. 10–17. What happened when Y. W. was teased? Why? (red card)	*Children of Wind and Water:* Read chapter 2, "A Dakota Hunter," to find out how the snow helped the hunters. Write in reading log. (yellow card)	*Mare for Young Wolf:* Write and format Mother's Day message for cards. (white card)
9:40	*Mare for Young Wolf:* Discuss chapter 2. What were Grandfather's lessons? (white card)	*Young Wolf's First Hunt:* Read the rest of chapter 2 to find what made father proud. Write in reading log. (red card)	*Children of Wind and Water:* Same as above. (yellow card)
10:00	*Children of Wind and Water:* Chapter 2, "A Dakota Hunter." Discuss how the snow helped the hunters. Review to find all the things that the Dakotas made from the buffalo. (yellow card)	*Mare for Young Wolf:* Read first four pages of chapter 3 to find out what Young Wolf's first idea was. Why did it work? Write in reading log. (white card)	*Young Wolf's First Hunt:* Same as above. (red card)

12-in.-by-16-in. pocket chart (a drawing of the pocket chart follows). Down the left-hand side were cards with meeting times. In the first time slot, I placed different-colored cards with the name of the book and the names of the students reading that book. The three columns across the top were labeled with the workstations: "Read With Teacher," "Independent Work," and "Computer Work." On those days when we had only two rotations, I flipped over the third meeting-time card. On the back, it read, "First group tomorrow." This indicated that students would begin the following day's session in the same column but would work on activities in the first time slot.

Space limitations prevent a detailed description of all the lessons that grew out of each book, but I include the book choice activity, a sample grammar lesson for one of the books, and a sample reading circle activity for each of the three main books. We were reading these books to gather information about lifestyles of different Native American tribes, so I planned to direct the reading with questions. I had observed when working on another unit that very few students in this class had confidence in their ability to get information from text. I asked questions before they read to assist them in understanding.

Pocket Chart

	Read w/teacher	Independent work	Computer
9:20	Y.W.F.H. Leranchona Jasmine Miguel Filsan Bumi [red card]	C.W.&W. Andrey Justin Dano Suada Christian [yellow card]	M.F.Y.U. Jesse Uilou Yvenie Linda Tamar [white card]
9:40	[white card]	[red card]	[yellow card]
10:00	[yellow card]	[white card]	[red card]

[on reverse:] first group tomorrow

This standard applies to all the reading circle activities that follow.

> **Goal 2, Standard 3** To use English to achieve academically in all content areas: Students will use appropriate learning strategies to construct and apply academic knowledge.

Descriptors

- applying basic reading comprehension skills such as skimming, scanning, previewing and reviewing text

- using context to construct meaning

- actively connecting new information to information previously learned

- evaluating one's own success in a completed learning task

Progress Indicators

- verbalize relationships between new information and information learned in another setting

- make a picture to check comprehension of a story or process

- rephrase, explain, revise, and expand oral or written information to check comprehension

Book Choice Activity

Although it is often difficult to find books for reading circles that all work into a unit of study, I was fortunate to find three books that were generally at the reading level of my students: *Children of the Wind and Water* (Krensky, 1994), *A Mare for Young Wolf* (Shefelman, 1993), and *Young Wolf's First Hunt* (Shefelman, 1995). My students found all of the books interesting, and I believe we made a lot of progress overcoming the discouraging month of testing (when more than one of my students had said in exasperation, "I hate reading!"). One of the groups was finishing its book faster than the others, so I found a fourth book, *Chief Joseph: Leader of Destiny* (Jassem, 1979). During the 6 weeks of the unit, all groups had an opportunity to read two of the books. Some of the students picked up extra copies and read them on their own.

Procedure

- On the first day of the unit, I gave the students brief descriptions of the three books we would be reading:

    1. *Children of the Wind and Water:* This book has five stories about Native American children from five different tribes. They tell a little about what life was like for children about 200 years ago.

    2. *A Mare for Young Wolf:* Young Wolf is a boy from a Plains tribe. The book is set in an era before contact with Europeans, but after Spanish horses had been introduced to the continent. Horses were important to the life of the tribe, and this book is about Young Wolf's first horse and how he learned to train her.

3. *Young Wolf's First Hunt:* Hunting buffalo was important and dangerous work in Young Wolf's tribe. He wanted to join the men in the hunt, but his father said he was too young. The book shows how Young Wolf found a way to go on the hunt.

- I passed out the books so that the students could read a page or two, look at the pictures, and decide which book they wanted to read. They then wrote their names on 3-in.-by-5-in. cards, along with their first, second, and third choices.

- I collected the cards and that evening put the students into groups; I took first choices into account, but if too many children wanted to read the same book, I took into consideration which children worked well together. We started our reading circles the following day.

> I keep track of whether students get their first, second, or third choice and always tell those that are placed with their third choice that they will be sure to get their first choice the next time. This cuts down on grumbling and cries of "No fair."

Children of the Wind and Water

Children of the Wind and Water (Krensky, 1994) lent itself well to comparisons of the lives of Muskogee, Dakota, Huron, Tlingit, and Nootka children.

PROCEDURE

- During reading circle and independent work, the students answered questions that touched on the differences among the tribes, such as "What was the difference between the way the Huron and Muskogee made their canoes?" "What foods did the Nootka eat? What did the Dakota eat? Why the difference?"

- When the group had read all five stories, the students made individual charts in which they compared lifestyles, homes, clothing, food, and the skills children learned.

> In an assignment in which the students had to use pictures from the book to describe the different tribes' houses, Dano noticed that the houses of the Muskogee had roofs like the houses of Kampuchea, where his family is from. He wrote: "The roof look like a house in Kampuchea and the flore and when it is summer you can stay cold and you can eat in their."

A Mare for Young Wolf

A Mare for Young Wolf (Shefelman, 1993) is well suited to plot analysis in that Young Wolf, on his own and with the help of his grandfather, is faced with a different problem to overcome in each chapter.

PROCEDURE

- Before we read the book, I asked the students to imagine what life would have been like for them if they had lived in America before the white man came. Miguel's paper about Young Wolf showed that he was able to imagine himself in this era and place, albeit as a modern Spanish-speaking boy who knows how to read (shown on p. 13).

Miguel's Paper

Young Wolf

If I lived befor the Europeans
Came it would be funer because
we could play in trees all the
times to get food. I would
play with Indinas boys. and when I grow
up I will go hunting with my
friends I would hunt deers and
buffalos for all the people
then we would go to the rever
My fiends will help me do cool.
he would teach me how to
read in Indin and i
would teach him how to read
in Spanch.

- For a summary of the book, the students wrote about the main problems in all of the chapters and how Young Wolf solved them. Filsan's Chapter-by-Chapter Problem Paper is shown on page 14.

- In one discussion of what Grandfather had taught Young Wolf, I wanted the students to understand that Grandfather was teaching a lesson when he told Young Wolf to find a way to solve the problem. I was especially excited when Filsan recognized my own teaching style in a conversation in which we were discussing Grandfather's teaching of Young Wolf.

Jorge: He said put his hands on [the horse he was training] and push hard.

Jasmine: When the boys call names, Grandfather say don't be mad.

Teacher: Now, read page 22 to find another way Grandfather is teaching him.

[As the students read, they began to look puzzled.]

Filsan: He didn't tell him nothing.

Jorge: The horse is afraid of Young Wolf.

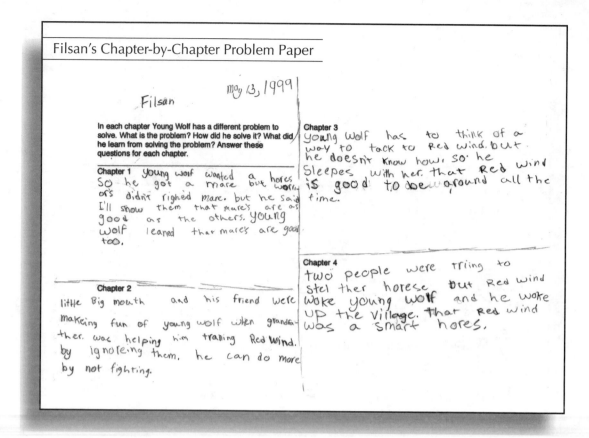

Filsan's Chapter-by-Chapter Problem Paper

Filsan   may 13, 1999

In each chapter Young Wolf has a different problem to solve. What is the problem? How did he solve it? What did he learn from solving the problem? Answer these questions for each chapter.

Chapter 1 young wolf wanted a hores so he got a mare but worrirors didn't righed mare. but he said I'll show them that mare's are as good as the others. young wolf leaned that mare's are good too.

Chapter 2
little Big mouth and his friend were makeing fun of young wolf when grandather was helping him traning Red Wind. by ignoreing them. he can do more by not fighting.

Chapter 3 young wolf has to think of a way to tack to Red wind. but he doesn't know how. so he sleepes with her. that Red wind is good to be around all the time.

Chapter 4
two people were triing to stel ther horese. but Red wind woke young wolf and he woke up the village. that Red wind was a smart hores.

Teacher: Did Grandfather tell him what to do?
Jorge: No . . .
Jasmine: He say [reading from book], "You will think of a way."
Teacher: Maybe Grandfather thinks he will learn better if he has to figure it out for himself.
Filsan: I know, Ms. Syvanen, that's how you teach us.

Young Wolf's First Hunt

In *Young Wolf's First Hunt* (Shefelman, 1995), Young Wolf is told that he is too young to go on the buffalo hunt. He, his horse, and a friend train in secret and then show that they know enough to join the hunt.

PROCEDURE

- When introducing the book, I said that Young Wolf wanted to show his family that he was old enough to go on the hunt and could do things as an adult.

- We then talked about what the students would do if they were adults that they could not do as children.

- As we read the book, the students kept a list of what Young Wolf did that showed he was becoming a man. Anna's list is shown on page 15.

Vocabulary and Grammar Teaching

I usually taught vocabulary and grammar in the context of the stories we were reading. Sometimes, in the process of that day's reading circle discussions, I would realize that students had not understood something. I would identify the troublesome item, perhaps

Anna's List

Anna

What were the things that
Young Wolf learned that were
important in becoming a man?
1. You have to be careful
2. Watch your life
3. It is hard to be a man
4. You can be scared to be a man
5. You have to be fast

a key word they did not understand or a grammatical structure they were not familiar with, and either do a minilesson right then or schedule it for the next day. What follows is one example of how I addressed these issues.

PROCEDURE

One day, we were reading about a young Muskogee girl, Sweet Water, who completed a transaction with a villager, with her father's approval. In the course of the discussion, it became obvious that the students had not understood that the trade had taken place. The part of the text that described this transaction (and that had confused the students) read, "Sweet Water looked to her father. The deerskins were soft and a rich brown color. With his approval, the trade was completed" (O'Dell & Hall, 1992, p. 8). The students understood the first two sentences, but they did not understand whose approval was needed. To maintain the flow of the story as we were reading it aloud together, I explained to the students what had happened.

- When we had finished reading the segment of the story for that day, I wrote the words *he, she, his,* and *her* on a piece of paper.
- I directed the students to go to the page where the whole of the trade is described and to skim the lines until they found one of the pronouns listed. As the students located the pronoun, I asked who that was and what he or she was doing.
- The students quickly learned to look to the beginning of the sentence or paragraph for the referent. When we had finished that section of the book, the students were much clearer about pronominal referents.

Computer Work

The third workstation during reading circle time was computer work. My goal for this activity was to familiarize the students with the computer, the keyboard, and word processing. Although the computer tasks were not usually related to the unit, they were all authentic writing activities that the students embarked on with great enthusiasm.

PROCEDURE

The students worked on the following assignments during the 6-week unit:

- Write a message for Mother's Day cards (in the native language whenever possible).

- Write a thank-you note to our volunteer on her last day.

- Write a letter to a favorite teacher who had moved away in the middle of the year.

- Write captions in the students' native languages for a bulletin board display.

- Type up the poem of the week and format it appropriately.

- Write a birthday message to the principal.

Assessment and Record Keeping

PROCEDURE

- For each reading circle, I made a folder. Inside were 3-in.-by-5-in. cards, one for each student, with the name of the student written at the bottom. Each card was attached to the folder with a strip of tape at the top so that the cards could be flipped up (see the drawing of my record-keeping folder, below). When students were in their reading circle, I made notes on their reading miscues and strategies. When we completed a book, I made notes for myself in which I summarized my observations. With these records, I could see patterns in the students' behavior, their reading strategies, and their reading needs. I was then able to plan instruction accordingly and make suggestions to the students. For example, I might suggest that students start reading more challenging books or books with which they would feel more comfortable. This system easily allowed me to keep track of the progress of each student. When the reading groups changed, I filed the cards in the individual students' folders.

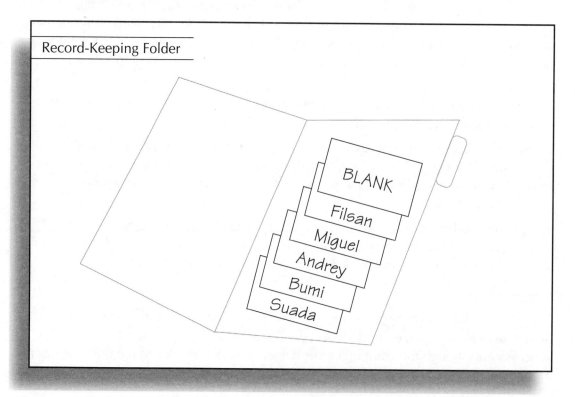

Record-Keeping Folder

- Each quarter I kept a more formal **running record** on each student's reading as part of our schoolwide assessment plan. Through a running record, I found that when Jesse read, he often made meaningful substitutions that were not phonetically close to the text. His homeroom teacher had arranged for a tutor for him because he was a struggling reader and his spelling was hard to decipher. I met with the tutor and pointed out how Jesse often preserved meaning even though he was not paying close attention to the graphophonic cues. It was clear that he was reading for meaning, not just calling out words. I asked the tutor not to correct his errors if they made sense, and to work on graphophonic awareness by asking him to write each session and teaching spelling strategies.

Other Activities

Film

Had You Lived Then: Life in the Woodlands Before the White Man Came (ACI Media, 1976) is a dramatization of a woodland Native American who lived before contact with Europeans. It shows him getting ready to hunt, stalking a deer, killing it, and then using the different parts of the deer. Many of the students in my class had gone hunting with their fathers or had heard stories from family members about hunting. This film provided us with material to make comparisons between life then and now.

> *Goal 2, Standard 2* **To use English to achieve academically in all content areas: Students will use English to obtain, process, construct, and provide subject matter information in spoken and written form.**
>
> ### Descriptors
> - comparing and contrasting information
> - listening to, speaking, reading, and writing about subject matter information
> - retelling information
> - representing information visually
>
> ### Progress Indicators
> - synthesize, analyze, and evaluate information
> - construct a chart synthesizing information

PROCEDURE

- We watched the film toward the beginning of the second week of the unit.
- Afterward, I asked a series of questions to help the students think about differences between life back then and life now. To elicit responses from all students, I started out by asking very open-ended questions, such as "What did you see in the movie?" "What happened?" As the students answered these questions, I acknowledged what they said and brought out more

details by asking additional questions, such as "Why was he moving so quietly when he was tracking the deer?"

- As we discussed what we had seen in the movie, I wrote new vocabulary, such as *tracking, bow and arrow,* and *wigwam,* on the overhead projector.

- Once I had established what the students had learned from the movie, we started a **Venn diagram**. We had used Venn diagrams earlier in the year, so the students were familiar with the concept. I started the process on the overhead projector by drawing two overlapping circles. The students supplied the circle names, *Centuries ago* and *Today.* In the overlapping section, I wrote *hunting deer.* The students then generated items to be placed in the *Centuries ago* circle, such as *used bow and arrow* and *walked to the place they hunted,* and the *Today* circle, such as *use guns* and *drive in a car.* They decided that at both times people ate the deer, but in the *Centuries ago* circle, we placed *main meat for people* and in the *Today* circle *some people eat a little* (deer). About 10 people in our class had tasted venison.

> So that all students can participate in the discussion period, I ask questions that can be answered either simply or in greater depth. For example, when I asked, "What did you see in the movie?" Suada, a beginner to English, responded, "Deer, man. Um, ah, um, ah," and then acted out shooting a bow and arrow. Jesse, a more fluent, upper-intermediate-level speaker of English, said, "A man hunting and he shoots a deer."

- After the demonstration, the students worked in pairs to finish their own diagrams.

ASSESSMENT

- As the students worked in pairs, I walked around, listening to discussions, observing progress on diagrams, and answering questions. Through these observations, I could see who understood the process and who was struggling.

- Some students, like Jesse and Justin, easily thought of more ideas for their Venn diagrams:

Jesse:	Let's do clothes [writing *clothes* in the overlap].
Justin:	[pointing to *Centuries ago*] Here made from deer and rabbit.
Jesse:	Today, jacket, T-shirt, jeans.

Some, like Andrey and Christian, struggled with the categories:

Andrey:	The boy killed the rabbit to eat, but I have a rabbit for a pet.
Christian:	[pointing to the overlap] Teacher, what we put here?

I directed the boys to write the thoughts in the categories of *Centuries ago* or *Today.* I then asked them what word was the same in both sentences. They then wrote *rabbits* in the overlap. I helped them get started on their next item and then moved on.

- Bumi and Suada were working on their diagram of beautifully overlapping circles very diligently, immersed in conversation. As they had no questions, I moved on. It was not until I had collected the papers that I saw that they had drawn the Venn diagram and written what they had seen in the movie in narrative form instead of in captions. I realized that the next time we worked on categorization, I would need to work more closely with them to make sure that they understood what the directions were and how to categorize.

Moccasin Making

On Fridays, I liked to make sure that we had some variety or some hands-on activities in our schedule. The students worked hard all week, and there was a school policy of no recess except for 15 minutes at lunchtime. I also wanted to see them work on problem solving with materials; they had been doing a lot of problem solving in math, but they had not had many opportunities to solve three-dimensional problems. At the end of the second week of the unit, I decided to ask the students to design and make their own moccasins.

It is important to offer open-ended, problem-solving activities to students in order to see how they function when using other types of intelligence. These activities reveal strengths in those students who do not shine in standard academic tasks. This type of activity gave me a lot of insight into my students' tolerance for ambiguity (those who begged me to show them how to do it appeared to have very little), ability to plan ahead (some used only one deerskin per shoe, and others depleted my cache of brown paper bags with their false starts), and spatial sense (all who were able to take their flat deer-skin to a finished shoe demonstrated this).

Goal 2, Standard 3 **To use English to achieve academically in all content areas: Students will use appropriate learning strategies to construct and apply academic knowledge.**

Descriptors

- applying basic reading comprehension skills such as skimming, scanning, previewing, and reviewing text
- using context to construct meaning
- actively connecting new information to information previously learned

Progress Indicators

- verbalize relationships between new information and information previously learned in another setting
- make pictures to check comprehension of a story or process
- rephrase, explain, revise, and expand oral or written information to check comprehension

PROCEDURE

- A few days after we had seen the movie *Had You Lived Then: Life in the Woodlands Before the White Man Came* (ACI Media, 1976), I asked the class to remember what Native Americans had made from deerskins. (We had listed items of clothing and types of shelter, wigwams and tipis.)

- I told the students that the shoes the Native Americans made were called *moccasins* and that I was going to give each student in the class a "deerskin" in the form of a brown paper grocery bag. They were to design a shoe that they could make from the deerskin provided. I substituted scissors for the bone or sharp rock knife and masking tape for the bone needle and deer tendons used for sewing.

- As the students set to work, I walked around observing. Some students got right to work cutting and taping. Others seemed to be at a loss as to where to begin. I assisted them by asking questions such as "What parts do you need in a shoe?" "How big does it need to be?" but I did not tell anyone how to make the moccasins. Some students worked closely with their neighbors. Others did their own work, talking to neighbors only when they needed scissors or tape.

Modern Native Americans

Most of the material that we had been reading was about Native Americans in the past. Part of my goal for the unit was to have the students also learn something about modern Native Americans. Several of the books that we had borrowed from the library covered life in the past as well as life today. Also, I had located a film on present-day Chippewa children (Atlantic Productions, 1975).

> ### *Goal 2, Standard 1*   To use English to achieve academically in all content areas: Students will use English to interact in the classroom.
>
> #### *Descriptors*
>
> - participating in full-class, group, and pair discussions
> - requesting information and assistance
> - negotiating and managing interaction to accomplish tasks
>
> #### *Progress Indicators*
>
> - request supplies to complete an assignment
> - take turns when speaking in a group
> - modify a statement made by a peer
> - paraphrase a teacher's directions orally or in writing

PROCEDURE

- At the beginning of the fifth week of the unit, we watched *An Indian Summer* (Atlantis Productions, 1975), about Chippewa children who live on a modern woodland reservation. The movie discusses their relationship with animals and the environment.

- In our discussion following the film, the students indicated that they saw the Chippewa children as being very much like themselves; differences they mentioned were mainly those grounded in urban and rural lifestyles. For example, the powwow portrayed in the film reminded them of getting together with other people from their ethnic groups to celebrate special holidays. Unlike the Chippewa children in the film, however, my students, as urban children, do not have the freedom to go far from home.

- The next day, I read *Buffalo Days* (Hoyt-Goldsmith, 1997) to the class. This book about a modern-day Crow boy is illustrated with photographs of him and his family living on a ranch on the Crow Reservation. The pictures of all-terrain vehicles and helicopters being used in rounding up the buffalo impressed us all, as we had not made the connection that buffalo still live. From our earlier reading, we remembered descriptions of the buffalo jumps used before horses were introduced to the Americas, and we had seen pictures of buffalo hunting with horses, but the existence of modern-day buffalo was a new concept for us all.

- The final pages of *Buffalo Days* were devoted to the Crow Fair and Rodeo, to which Crow come from all around and camp at the fairgrounds. Many people were camping in tipis at the encampment. It was at this point that the students asked if they could make little tipis like the ones they had seen in *Indians of the Plains* (Thomson, 1991). We compared pictures and descriptions in books on traditional tipis. At the end of the week, I brought in "buffalo hides" (brown paper grocery bags) and "poles" (bamboo garden stakes), and we made tipis following a pattern in *Indians of the Plains*.

Culminating Activity

I wanted the culminating activity to reflect my goals for the unit, which had not been tied to learning discrete bits of information but were intended to help my students develop an understanding of the range of cultures represented by Native Americans. Rather than channeling their energies into a project I had planned, I asked the students to decide what they wanted to do as a culminating activity. They also wrote an end-of-unit reflection and completed a self-assessment. The culminating activities lasted for the entire last week of the unit.

Goal 2, Standard 2   **To use English to achieve academically in all content areas: Students will use English to obtain, process, construct, and provide subject matter information in spoken and written form.**

Descriptors

- listening to, speaking, reading, and writing about subject matter information
- retelling information
- selecting, connecting, and explaining information

Progress Indicators

- use information from a number of sources to construct dioramas
- make an oral presentation to classmates

Goal 2, Standard 3 To use English to achieve academically in all content areas: Students will use appropriate learning strategies to construct and apply academic knowledge.

Descriptor

• evaluating one's own success in a completed learning task

Progress Indicators

• write a self-evaluation
• write a reflection on what was learned

PROCEDURE

• I introduced the culminating activity by telling the class that they would be doing an end-of-unit project that would illustrate some of what they had learned. Earlier in the year, our culminating projects had taken the form of bulletin board displays, class books, dioramas, and oral reports. I reminded them of all the sources of information we had been working with, such as the read-aloud book, reading circle books, library books, and films. I also reminded them of the kinds of culminating activities we had done during the year. I then asked them what they would like to do for this unit. As the students made their suggestions, I wrote them on the overhead projector. Soon individual students began choosing their activities.

• When the discussion ended, most students wanted to make dioramas, and they decided to work in three groups. Dano organized a group that made Muskogee-style houses, including items that were important to the Muskogee, such as the platform inside houses, pots, and deerskins. Yvenie's group made tipis and decorated them with items that were important to Native Americans of the Plains. Andrey and his group worked at building North West Coast–style long houses out of Popsicle sticks and drawing totems. Miguel, a fifth grader, worked alone on a speech about Chief Joseph.

> Fifth graders in the state of Oregon are required to successfully deliver a speech in their classrooms as part of the fifth-grade benchmark in speaking, which is rated by the classroom teacher using a state-developed scoring guide. I was pleased to see Miguel apply what we had been learning in our class to the work in his regular education classroom.

• During the week that the students were working on their projects, they were also working on their end-of-unit reflections. They had three questions to answer:

1. What did you learn in your readings on Native Americans?

2. What was the most interesting thing you learned?

3. Why do you think this was the most interesting?

We had discussed these questions in the reading circles to prepare the students for this reflection.

- On the last day of the unit, the students gave brief reports on either their end-of-unit reflections or their culminating activities.

At the end of units, I often ask students to give reports to help prepare them for the more daunting task of giving oral reports in their regular education classrooms.

- After the students had given their reports, they completed a self-assessment. I asked them to look back over all that they had worked on during this unit. (They stored all their papers in their reading logs, which had pockets for loose papers.) In this self-assessment, they listed the books they read in their reading circles, remarked on the themes of the books and what they had learned from them, and then rated themselves on the quality of their work and the effort they had put into it. Anna's and Miguel's self-assessment forms are shown on the next page.

RESOURCES

Books for Children and Young Adults

Baylor, B. (1974). *They put on masks.* New York: Charles Scribner's Sons.
   In this beautifully illustrated book, the author describes different purposes for masks among Native American tribes.

Freedman, R. (1994). *An Indian winter.* New York: Scholastic.
   In the winter of 1833–1834, two Europeans stayed with the Mandan in what is now North Dakota. Freedman has adapted parts of the journal of Alexander Philippe Maximilian to make it more readable for today's young readers. The book is illustrated with the sketches and paintings of Karl Bodmer.

Hoyt-Goldsmith, D. (1997). *Buffalo days.* New York: Holiday House.
   This book tells the story of a modern Crow boy and his life on his parents' ranch on the Crow reservation. It tells about the efforts by the Crow to reestablish wild buffalo herds.

Jassem, K. (1979). *Chief Joseph: Leader of destiny.* Mahwah, NJ: Troll Associates.
   This biography of Chief Joseph begins with his childhood and ends with his surrender to General Howard and his "I will fight no more forever" speech.

Krensky, S. (1991). *Children of the earth and sky.* New York: Scholastic.
   These five stories about Native American children of the Hopi, Comanche, Mohican, Navajo, and Mandan tribes describe typical skills those children would learn.

Krensky, S. (1994). *Children of the wind and water.* New York: Scholastic.
   These five stories about Native American children of the Muskogee, Dakota, Heron, Tlingit, and Nootka tribes describe typical skills those children would learn.

McConkey, L. (1973). *Sea and cedar: How the North West Coast Indians lived.* Seattle, WA: Madrona Press.
   The illustrations and text show the houses, clothing, tools, and totems of the North West Coast Indians.

O'Dell, S., & Hall, E. (1992). *Thunder rolling in the mountains.* New York: Dell.
   This book is written from the point of view of Sound of Running Feet, the 14-year-old daughter of Chief Joseph of the Nez Perce. It begins with the Nez Perce's move from their traditional home in the Wallowa Mountains, and continues through Chief Joseph's surrender and famous speech, "I will fight no more forever."

Self-Assessments

Name Anna   Date 5-11-99

I read Young Wolf's fast Hunt

This book was about How to be a man

I learned to be come a man is hard.

(I did all) most / some / none of the writing assignments.

I think this book was too easy (just right) too hard for me.

Looking at my reading log I would say that I did a poor / good / very good / (excellent job.)

I think you did an excellent job!

Name Miguel   Date 5-11-99

I read young wolf

This book was about how To be a Man

I learned To face all That you are afraid of.

(I did all) most / some / none of the writing assignments.

I think this book was too easy (just right) too hard for me.

Looking at my reading log I would say that I did a poor / good (very good) excellent job.

Penner, L. R. (1994). *The true story of Pocahontas.* New York: Random House.
    This easy-to-read book touches on aspects of Pocahontas's life from her childhood to her death in England. The conflicts between Native Americans and Europeans are covered, but teachers may need to supply background information for greater understanding. The book portrays Pocahontas's life more accurately than the popular movie does.

Roop, P., & Roop, C. (1992). . . . *If you lived with the Cherokee.* New York: Scholastic.
    This book describes what it would have been like to live with the Cherokee about 200 years ago. The book effectively draws students in through the use of a predictable element—"If you were a child, you would . . ."—to present information. If I had had more time to collect a set, I would have used this book for a reading circle.

Shefelman, J. (1993). *A mare for Young Wolf.* New York: Random House.

Young Wolf is a Comanche boy who is old enough to have his own horse. He picks a mare, not usually a boy's horse, but learns to train his horse, and they both prove themselves worthy.

Shefelman, J. (1995). *Young Wolf's first hunt.* New York: Random House.

Young Wolf wants to go on a buffalo hunt, but his father says that he is not old enough. In secret, Young Wolf and a friend teach themselves and their horses to hunt so that they can join the older boys and men in the next hunt.

Shemie, B. (1991). *Houses of hide and earth.* Montreal, Canada: Tundra Books.

This small book has clear pictures and simple text that describe the earth houses and tipis of the Plains Indians.

Thomson, R. (1991). *Indians of the plains.* New York: Franklin Watts.

My students enjoyed this book because of the crafts, sign language illustrations, and picture writing. We used the directions to make tipis.

Westridge Young Writers Workshop. (1995). *Kids explore the heritage of western Native Americans.* Santa Fe, NM: John Muir.

Books written by children are accessible to ESOL students. These stories from six Indian nations include history, descriptions of present-day life, and Native American arts and crafts. It is a good resource book.

Wood, L. (1994). *Child rearing.* Vero Beach, FL: Rourke.

Historical and modern photographs of Native Americans are used to illustrate and compare past and present child-rearing practices in several tribes.

Films

ACI Media (Producer). (1976). *Had you lived then: Life in the woodlands before the White man came* [Film]. (Available from Aims Media, 6901 Woodley Avenue, Van Nuys, CA 91406)

This 12-minute film depicts the importance of deer in the survival of early North American natives.

Atlantis Productions (Producer). (1975). *An Indian summer* [Film]. (Available from Atlantis Productions, Inc., 1252 LaGranada Drive, Thousand Oaks, CA 91360)

This 11-minute film portrays a summer experience of Chippewa children on a woodland reservation, including their relationship with animals and the environment.

Wolper Productions (Producer). (1975). *I will fight no more forever* [Film]. (Available from Library Video Company, P.O. Box 580, Catalog M-63, Wynnewood, PA 19096)

This 106-minute film is a dramatization of the 1877 flight of Chief Joseph and his small band of Nez Perce from U.S. government troops attempting to place the tribe on a reservation. The running fight lasted for more than 11 weeks and covered 1,600 miles before Chief Joseph was caught just 40 miles from the Canadian border.

Work Cited

TESOL. (1997). *ESL standards for pre-K–12 students.* Alexandria, VA: Author.

UNIT 2
Writing for Each Other

JIM HUGHES

Introduction

A child was crying. I was on recess duty, the second day of school. The boy was of the Mien tribe, a farming people from Laos. "Why are you crying?" I asked, bending at the waist. He looked to me as if he were a second grader. I got down on one knee. "What's the matter?" His tears kept flowing. "Are you hurt?" I asked, seeing no visible wound. He nodded, his breath short and violent now with sobs. "Where are you hurt?" He tried to answer, but I did not understand him. English was his second language, so I was not surprised that I did not comprehend his words, especially when he was crying.

The bell rang to go in. Frustrated with my lack of progress, I decided his teacher would have to deal with his problem. "Who is your teacher?" I asked. His crying, which was abating, gathered strength. "Who is your teacher?" I demanded, angry that he wouldn't help me. "Just tell me! Who is your teacher?" "You, Mr. Hughes!" he shouted. "YOU!"

My class and I had various maxims that reflected our way of looking at learning and at each other. Most of them were made up on the spot as occasion dictated. One came about because of how hard it was for many of my students to face up to their mistakes or

---

Context

Grade level: Third grade

English proficiency level: Beginning to advanced; native speakers

Native language of students: English (including a nonstandard dialect, Ebonics), Kabyle (a Berber language), Lao, Mien, Punjabi, Spanish, Tagalog

Focus of instruction: Writing and social studies (ethnicity, family history, geography)

Type of class: Mainstream, self-contained multiracial class of 20 students, including 12 ESOL students

Length of unit: 4 weeks

failures. It was "We like our mistakes because we can learn from them." After my encounter with this Mien boy, I made up a new maxim: "There are mistakes, and there are MISTAKES." I was devastated, and I shudder to think what injury I did to that child. Out of that experience, however, my whole way of teaching was transformed, and it led me to the unit I wish to share with you.

The year of the MISTAKE, I had 31 children in my class, and that first week I was getting to know names and associating them with faces. I now realize my motive was primarily a management one, for if I knew their names, I thought I could (maybe) control them. I had "identity affirmation" projects, such as the "me T-shirt" designed to show their favorite place, activity, food, and TV show or video game. These activities were all well and good but rather superficial. Although I appeared to be learning about the children, I was not "digging down deep," nor was I revealing anything about myself.

To be honest, class management was my major concern, not only because of behavioral problems; the sheer number of students seemed to demand it. Also, I was the only White person in the room. Most of these third-grade children were Black, many were Latino, and a few were Asian American. I was unsure how they and their parents regarded me and what I might expect of them. My task, as I then saw it, was to establish order: structures, routines, expectations, authority (mine), and responsibility (theirs).

If this preoccupation with order seems reprehensible, let me emphasize that, although what I did appeared necessary, reasonable, and commonplace, I did not like it. In fact, I was contemplating a career change because I had found teaching to be disheartening. My passion was creative writing, but my mistake that fateful day did not hasten my departure from teaching; rather, it made me reflect on my teaching practice. I realized that, to be meaningful for my students and for me, the teaching process had to become similar to the writing practice I was already cultivating.

When I write fiction, I need to be receptive to my voice. It might delight me, or it might surprise or shock me. In any case, I have to give it its chance, encourage its fluency and content, and permit it to establish its own structures, rhythms, and tones. My job as a writer is to facilitate its expression and, because writing for an audience is communication, help it master the conventions of language, such as spelling and punctuation, so it can be read and understood.

The analogy with teaching fell into place. I realized that when I taught, especially when I taught writing, I needed to be receptive to my students' voices. Because these voices were not only unique but also had cultural, social, historical, and geographical resonances foreign to me, I could learn as much from my students as they could from me. I realized that my task as a teacher was to facilitate my students' self-expression, guide them toward a mastery of standard English, and stimulate explorations of their backgrounds.

I was fortunate that two unforeseen occurrences favored my plan. One was the arrival of a new principal who was 100% behind my vision, having a similar one himself, and who gave me valuable suggestions and encouragement. The other was class-size reduction, which limited my class to 20 students, making it easier to actualize my ideas.

I now had a new priority for the first weeks: Get to know each student. Never again would I fail to recognize one of my own students! But how? Private conferences? What would the rest of the class do? What if a student were shy, intimidated by a new teacher, or had limited communication skills in English? Would one 10-minute conference be sufficient? Might it require more interviews? More time? I needed an intimate, but public, inclusive forum. I hit upon the idea of establishing a daily class circle at which I would get to know each student and the children would get to know each other and me.

The daily class circle was good class management. It also nurtured a learning environment in which we were all engaged. Moreover, it built a sense of community. We became a community of learners and creators, of which I was a member. The atmosphere was one of mutual respect and trust, and we regarded risk taking as heroic.

The structure was now in place. But what about the content? How would we get to know one another, not only as individuals, but also as social, cultural, and historical people who had geographical roots different from the landscape we now shared in northern California? My answer to this question was to develop this unit.

Unit Overview

I intended "Writing for Each Other" to last 4 weeks. We continued, however, to draw inspiration from the activity throughout the year. In what follows, I share its beginnings in that first month of school. The focus of instruction was writing and social studies,

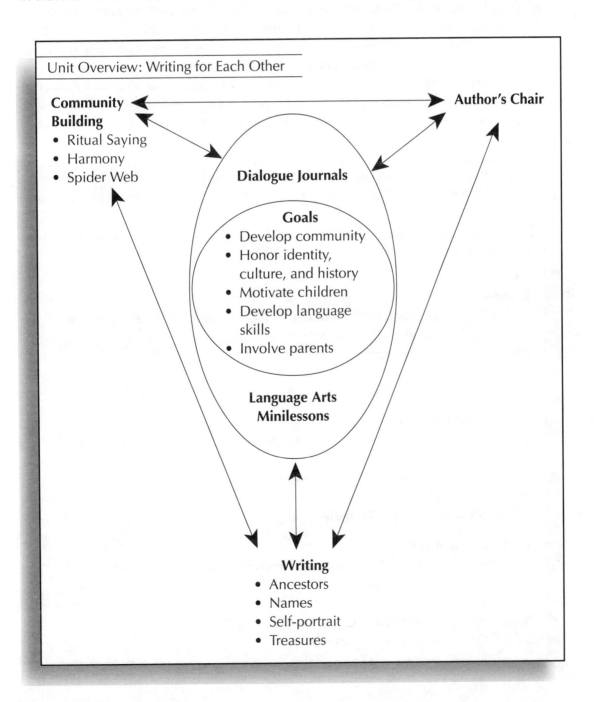

Unit Overview: Writing for Each Other

Community Building
- Ritual Saying
- Harmony
- Spider Web

Author's Chair

Dialogue Journals

Goals
- Develop community
- Honor identity, culture, and history
- Motivate children
- Develop language skills
- Involve parents

Language Arts Minilessons

Writing
- Ancestors
- Names
- Self-portrait
- Treasures

supported by community building and language development activities. My overarching goals were to

- develop a community of learners and creators
- honor each student's identity, culture, and history
- motivate the children, through the use of meaningful subject matter and author's chair, to achieve academically and mature socially
- develop my students' speaking, listening, reading, and writing skills
- involve my students' parents in their children's schooling

The unit overview on page 29 shows the relationship of these goals and the unit activities.

The early morning schedule, shown below, details the sequencing of activities and time allocations in the unit. The fact that the morning schedule was predictable was particularly helpful to the ESOL students as the structure of each day became familiar. On the rug, we chanted a ritual saying, then performed another community-building activity, such as Harmony or Spider Web (see pp. 33 and 34 for descriptions of these activities). After that, we immersed ourselves in the heart of the unit, listening and responding to class members' writing. By this time, the children had been on the rug for 40–60 minutes, so I had them go to tables and write in dialogue journals, which I responded to by the next day (see p. 47 and the glossary for a complete description of the procedure for implementing dialogue journals). After that, we returned to the rug, and I taught a language arts minilesson.

The writing topic changed each week, and during this 4-week unit, we explored and wrote about ancestors, names, self-portraits, and treasures. From the start, even my

---

Early Morning Schedule

Monday

8:30–9:00	Opening and community-building activities: ritual saying and Spider Web
9:00–9:20	Writing for each other: brainstorm week's topic
9:20–9:40	Dialogue journals
9:40–10:00	Language arts minilesson

Tuesday and Thursday

8:30–8:40	Opening and community-building activities: ritual saying and harmony
8:40–9:10	Author's chair (five students)
9:10–9:30	Dialogue journals
9:30–9:50	Language arts minilesson

Wednesday and Friday

8:30–8:40	Opening and community-building activities: ritual saying and spider web
8:40–9:10	Author's chair (five students)
9:10–9:30	Dialogue journals
9:30–9:50	Language arts minilesson

beginning-level ESOL students did not demonstrate either writing inhibitions or distaste for writing, probably because of positive writing experiences in lower grades. I made only one adaptation for English language learners: 25 minutes of English language development (ELD) from 10:35 to 11:00 each morning.

After introducing a writing assignment, I devoted an ELD session to making sure the ESOL students understood it. I repeated the instructions and examples, explained what was expected of the children, and gave them the opportunity to ask questions. If I saw the need, and if there were students who spoke the same language, I encouraged them to get clarification from their peers. In addition, I explored the ESOL students' background knowledge of the topic, recording their contributions on chart paper.

The next day, as support for the particular subject we were writing and reading about that week, we worked on vocabulary, often using a picture dictionary and realia. I wrote a word that was central to the assignment on chart paper (e.g., *heirloom*), and from it the English language learners constructed a word web based on any associations the central word suggested. Throughout the ELD lessons, I assessed my ESOL students' English language abilities by observing their participation in the various activities.

Throughout the unit, I performed ongoing assessments (largely observations) to determine how well the children and their parents were meeting my objectives. Because the writing assignments were homework and encouraged collaboration with family members, I could not be certain that the students did all their own writing. Therefore, during this first month of school, I relied on daily dialogue journal entries for writing appraisals. I did not correct the children's entries; I only responded to them. But I kept anecdotal records that enabled me to plan minilessons to support the students' interests, concerns, and enthusiasms, and to address standard English needs that most of the children seemed ready to incorporate into their writing. Later in the year, after I introduced writers' workshop, each student's writing, from first draft to publication, was class work, which enabled me to use it for formative assessment.

Standards

Why did the word *standards* give me the willies? Was I peculiar? From my conversations with other teachers, it did not appear so. One reason for my reaction was the word's meanings. It suggested an official rule for measuring and judging, an authoritative model for practice, and a mandatory level of attainment for the measure of adequacy. How imperial and dogmatic! Standards also suggested conformity to what was typical, having nothing to do with the special or extraordinary. How mediocre and bland!

A second reason for my negative reaction was similar to my dislike of class management as a chief preoccupation. Standards—this time directed at me as well as my students from an authority outside of my school or classroom—did not derive from the needs of my students and had little to do with the excitement of the learning process. I had had some experience with standards as the state of California had frameworks, which were standards of a sort but were quite vague. From our district, we had grade-level expectations, which managed to be vague and too specific at times. We had no ESL standards, though the district's bilingual office personnel would observe us now and then to make sure we were in compliance with California's ELD requirements. We also had *standard*ized tests, which gave us an idea of what our students were expected to know. That was about it. None of these documents really tapped into my students' needs as learners or my needs as a teacher, so standards were not high on my reading list earlier in my career.

I began to entertain the thought that standards might be useful when, in response to a state-required program quality review (PQR), my school decided to focus on improving writing. In the process of developing writing standards and a writing rubric, we became much more aware of what good writing was. Then, as a support provider for beginning teachers, I was presented with the *California Standards for the Teaching Profession* (State of California, 1997), a well-considered, thoughtful document that was valuable in improving my own teaching, as well as in supporting beginning teachers. These standards were intended to prompt reflection, improve teaching practice, and assess progress, and they did all of that for me.

Later still, I was introduced to *ESL Standards for Pre-K–12 Students* (TESOL, 1997), which I found useful as an instrument to

- broaden and deepen my understanding of the sorts of experiences, social and academic, English language learners needed

- stimulate ideas for lessons and activities

- assess the progress of my English language learners

These ESL standards for instruction and assessment appeared to me to arise from good teaching practice. I began to think of standards as a way to encourage and judge quality.

Community-Building Activities

I knew that it was important for us to develop a sense of community from the first day of school if we were to have a successful year. To that end, we devoted 5 minutes daily to a ritual saying and discussion of its meaning. I also knew that important components in the life of a community are for each member to get to know the others as soon as possible and learn to work cooperatively with them. Therefore, we spent 5–20 minutes each morning on one of two activities, Harmony or Spider Web, both designed to build a harmonious community.

Ritual Saying

Each morning, while sitting on the rug in our class circle, we recited a saying that underscored that, although each of us was a unique person and had our own cultural and historical background, we shared much in common. I encountered the ritual saying in the children's novel *Tamika and the Wisdom Rings* (Yarbrough, 1994, pp. 7–10) and adapted it for the purpose of reminding my students of our unity.

> **Goal 1, Standard 3** **To use English to communicate in social settings: Students will use learning strategies to extend their communicative competence.**
>
> ***Descriptor***
> - listening to and imitating how others use English
>
> ***Progress Indicator***
> - recite an opening saying with appropriate gestures

PROCEDURE

- Every morning, we sat in our class circle and recited the following ritual saying:

    We are born of an old seed. We are growing from a deep root. We are part of strong branches. We are the sweet fruit of the African or Latino or Asian or European or Native American branches of the human family tree. Wherever we may go, wherever we may be, I am part of you, you are part of me.

- We accompanied the recitation with gestures. First, we held our folded hands in front of us to represent the "old seed." Then we crossed our wrists and, with fingers outstretched, touched the floor to represent the "deep root." Next, we raised our arms to represent the "strong branches." Then we relaxed our wrists and let our hands droop to represent "sweet fruit." Next, we formed our arms into the shape of the globe while reciting, "Wherever we may go, wherever we may be." Then, after touching our chests, we gestured towards the whole group while reciting, "I am part of you." Finally, we brought our hands back to our chests while saying, "You are part of me."

ASSESSMENT

I assessed the effectiveness of this ritual with my ESOL students, in particular, by observing each day the children's verbal and nonverbal participation, and by asking questions that required them to tell what meaning, both literal and symbolic, they were taking from the ritual and how it might relate to the way they thought about and treated classmates.

Harmony

On the first day of school, I wished to make immediate contact with each student. At the very least, I thought, I would know their faces, even if I had not mastered their names! Harmony had two purposes: (a) to cultivate my bond with each of the students and (b) to build community by developing the children's cooperative skills.

This activity permitted us at the outset to act together cooperatively to produce a result. It was an initiation into our community of learners and creators. I was director, but also part of the community. We performed Harmony twice a week for the first month, then intermittently throughout the year. On the final day of school, the children asked if we could do it one last time.

Goal 1, Standard 1   **To use English to communicate in social settings: Students will use English to participate in social interactions.**

Descriptor
- using nonverbal communication in social interactions

Progress Indicator
- engage successfully in a nonverbal activity

PROCEDURE

- We sat in our class circle. I announced that no one should make a sound during the activity. I explained that each child was to start doing what I was doing when I looked him or her in the eyes.

- I rubbed my hands together and looked at Danielle, who was on my left. Once she started rubbing, I proceeded to the next child, continuing around the circle. When I returned to Danielle, I clapped my hands. When I was halfway around the circle, class members were making one of two sounds (rubbing or clapping). Once I got back to Danielle, I started to slap my thighs. The fourth time around, we pounded the floor with our palms.

- Once I had returned again to Danielle, I reversed the sequence of sounds (pounding palms on the floor, slapping thighs, clapping hands, rubbing hands).

- Once the entire class had joined in all the sounds, we stopped and were silent.

- I asked the students what they had imagined while they were making the sounds. Some had been thinking of horses walking, trotting, galloping, or running, but most said, "A rainstorm or thunderstorm."

ASSESSMENT

I assessed the effectiveness of this activity by observing whether the students, particularly the ESOL students, followed my verbal and nonverbal directions. If they did not, I observed whether they were able to pick up the nonverbal cues of the students who were performing successfully. I also observed their progress in mastering the activity on subsequent days.

Spider Web

The purpose of this third community-building activity was for us to get to know each other while fostering a nurturing and supportive learning environment, one in which all members were dependent on each other. We did Spider Web three times a week during this 4-week unit.

> **Goal 2, Standard 2**   To use English to achieve academically in all content areas: Students will use English to obtain, process, construct, and provide subject matter information in spoken and written form.
>
> **Descriptors**
> - gathering information orally
> - representing information visually
>
> **Progress Indicator**
> - construct a chart showing data

PROCEDURE

- We sat in our class circle. I announced that we would each tell what we most wanted to study about. I took a ball of yarn and said, "My name is Mr. Hughes, and I want to learn about whales."

- Next I held the end of the yarn and threw the ball, which unraveled as it flew, to Karina. She caught the ball of yarn and said, "My name is Karina, and I want to learn about planets." Then she held the strand of yarn and threw the ball to Jagjit, who continued the pattern. When everyone had had a turn, we stopped.

- We played with the web, discovering that if we plucked one strand, the whole web vibrated. At one point, a student got tangled in it, nearly spoiling it for us all.

- After discussing what the class had learned about community building from this activity, we collaboratively made up a maxim: "Our community is like a web. It is made up of human connections for which we are all responsible. Disrupt the web, and the spider will suck out your blood!"

  I often use classroom-based events and conversations to introduce new concepts. Later, I used this experience with the yarn and the maxim to introduce the children to genres. The first genre we talked about was the cautionary tale!

- We copied what the students most wanted to learn onto chart paper and displayed it on the closet doors. (These interests formed the basis of our next unit as the students researched their topics and wrote reports.) We also categorized the topics (e.g., animals, the universe), tallied the number of topics in each category, and constructed a bar graph to visually organize the data and show the popularity of the various categories.

- Each time we did Spider Web, we varied the content being explored. Topics included "My Oldest Living Relative," "Languages I Speak," "How I Got My Name and Nickname (if Any)," "What Similes I Would Use to Describe the Features of Mr. Hughes' Face," and "An Object I Treasure." Later in the year, the children sometimes suggested topics, such as "My Favorite Toy" and "A School Rule We Could Do Without."

ASSESSMENT

To be honest, I was disappointed with the topics the students selected, for only one had anything to do with ethnicity, family history, or geography (the themes of my projected unit). But I realized afterwards that mine did not either! Most students had chosen animals. It appeared that once I said "whales," the children started thinking in terms of animals, so that after Karina chose planets, Jagjit selected horses, Nai Hin chose sharks, and so on. However, Jeremy chose history. I asked, "Any special time in history?" He answered, "I want to know everything." "Great!" I exclaimed. "You can learn all the history you have time for." Ah, the joy of children such as Jeremy!

I decided that the next time I used this activity I would make sure to demonstrate better by selecting a more relevant topic. I also decided that it would be helpful to brainstorm first with the class, listing as many possibilities as we could. In this way, I hoped that the students would have a richer menu from which to choose.

By selecting history as his topic, Jeremy gave me an opening for our unit. I said, "Let's begin our year with Jeremy's idea. We'll research history—our family histories." In this way, we moved into the writing activities involving teacher-student-parent collaboration that were at the heart of this unit.

When assessing the success of Spider Web, I observed

- how well the students, especially the ESOL students, followed my verbal and nonverbal directions and the examples of their classmates

- how original, rather than derivative, their contributions were when the topic lent itself to choice

- how cooperative they were in creating and supporting the web

- how well they constructed bar graphs to represent class data, which I collected and put in their math portfolios in order to monitor their progress

Writing Activities: Writing for Each Other

The heart of this unit was the writing activities. I had several objectives. One was to improve my students' writing and other literacy skills to help them succeed in school. Another was to develop their self-esteem. A third was to build community within my class and with parents. My school was located in a low-income neighborhood, and parents did not usually feel comfortable with or welcomed at school. In my 12 years at the school, we had never been able to form a parent-teacher association or have much parent participation in school activities. I wished to create the conditions for the parents of my students to participate meaningfully and successfully in their children's schooling; I hoped that these writing assignments would help accomplish that goal.

I told the children that we were writing for each other, emphasizing two reasons for doing so:

- to establish that this was a sharing enterprise during which we would get to know and become more comfortable with each other as learners and creators

- to increase the quality of the students' writing; because we had public readings and the children knew classmates were their audience, it was more likely that they would try their best

In the following months, as writers' workshop developed, I generally did not assign writing topics, and students wrote, conferred, and completed their pieces at different times. In this unit, however, I assigned open-ended topics so that the children could, at the outset, learn about each other and their respective cultures. I expected the students to complete first drafts by the next day. This was because I needed to assign other homework (reading and math) during the week and wanted to restrict this assignment to one evening's work. I did not intend the students to take this piece of writing through several drafts, as they did in other situations. My goal was for them to write a draft, read it to their classmates, and receive oral responses from them and from me. This was primarily a sharing enterprise in which, through writing, students, parents, and I were communicating with and getting to know each other. For dialogue journal entries, however, children chose their own topics.

This standard applies to the general procedure and the four specific activities that are described here.

> **Goal 2, Standard 2**   To use English to achieve academically in all content areas: Students will use English to obtain, process, construct, and provide subject matter information in spoken and written form.

Descriptors

- listening to, speaking, reading, and writing about ethnicity, family history, and geography
- responding to the work of peers
- representing information visually
- formulating and asking questions

Progress Indicators

- volunteer information and respond to questions about self and family
- generate and ask questions of family member experts

PROCEDURE

- Each Monday, I assigned a writing topic that would allow us to learn about one another. Every week-long writing activity involved the following four elements or steps:

  1. We brainstormed about the subject in class for about 20 minutes. I recorded the students' ideas on chart paper, which I posted in the classroom.

  2. I always did the assignment myself, first, and then shared my "homework" with my students. This demonstrated what I expected while also sharing myself with them.

  3. I wrote a letter to the parents in which I explained the homework, enclosed the sample I had done, and thanked them for any help they could give their child. The students did the written assignment at home, with (I hoped) their parents or other family members, and brought their first drafts to school the following day.

  4. On Tuesdays through Fridays, five students each day read their writing to the entire class. We called this **author's chair**. Following the reading of a piece, the rest of the class asked questions or made comments. Each reading and peer and teacher response took about 5 minutes, so author's chair lasted about 25–30 minutes. Author's chair was a time for me to model and for the children to learn how to respond to writing without destroying the writer. Remarks had to be positive and helpful. I was very strict about this, immediately reacting to negative responses by pointing out why they were inappropriate because, from my experience with adult writing groups, I knew excellent writers who had given up writing because of destructive criticism. Often the students monitored each other, bringing peer pressure to bear on negative remarks and reminding each other of our maxim, which ended with, "The spider will suck

out your blood." If some students did not get it, I took them aside for a private conference. If many students acted improperly, I taught a minilesson.

- I did not assess these writings because I could not be sure that the students had written them by themselves. But I celebrated the students' accomplishments in the hope of motivating them to believe in their abilities and to continue to give their best efforts.

- We posted students' writing on a bulletin board unless they objected. I found that, although a few students were shy about their writing and sometimes reluctant to read it themselves, no one ever objected to it being read by a classmate or me or displayed for all to see.

Ancestors

Our first writing topic was *ancestors*. Two of my objectives for this assignment were to give students a topic about which they could obtain information easily (in most cases) and that would be relevant and meaningful to them. I also had purposes that related to my students' parents. I wished to introduce myself, begin a year-long communication with them, signify to them (and to their children) that I was interested in and respectful of their life stories and those of their ancestors, and involve them and other family members in their child's homework by assigning a topic that required the child to use family members as resources; indeed, I even requested that they write! In this way, I integrated academic goals for the students and community-building goals for students, their family members, and me.

PROCEDURE

- As a class, we brainstormed what the term *ancestors* meant. Because we could not agree, we went to the dictionary to look up the definition. In order to be as inclusive as possible, we broadened the definition to include living family members. In this way, *ancestors* came to mean parents, grandparents, great-grandparents, and so on.

- I explained to the students that I wanted them to write everything they knew about their parents. I also asked the children to ask their parents, grandparents, and great-grandparents to write everything they knew about their own parents.

- I read to the students what I had written about my ancestors and told them I was sending this information home in a letter to their parents. Because I was asking students, parents, and other family members to reveal facts about their lives, I felt it only fair that I reveal facts about my own. I believed, too, that this kind of self-disclosure would encourage families to respond. Also, I thought that my "homework" might serve as a model for everyone. My letter to parents follows:

> This week we are discussing ancestors. [Here I repeated the instructions I gave to the students.]
>
> I do not want in any way to invade your privacy, so please don't write anything you don't want made public.
>
> I think it only fair that I tell you about my ancestors. My mother was born in Southern California, my father in Missouri. My mother was a teacher, and my father was a mechanical engineer.

My mother's mother was born in Los Angeles in 1879. My mother's father was born in Canada and came to California about 1900. He grew oranges, lemons, and grapefruit. My father's parents were born in the South. His father worked for the railroad.

My son did a report on his ancestors when he was in the 7th grade. I learned many things. One was that my ancestors on my father's side were from Wales in Great Britain. The name Hughes means son of Hugh.

My ancestors on my mother's side were from Scotland and Ireland. They fled to America because my mother's great, great, etc., grandfather killed an unjust landlord. In Virginia, one of their children was kidnaped by Indians, but they got her back unharmed. It had been a misunderstanding—the excessive zeal of a suitor.

Thank you for your help with this assignment. I hope it's fun.

- Marilou, an intermediate-level ESOL student, wrote and read to us about not only her parents, but her grandparents as well:

Both of my parets were born in the Philippines. Both of them had business and my Dad Arceo had a rice field and mango farm. My Dad passed away when he was 38 and that was two and a half years ago and a few months before we (my mother, brother, and sister) came here in the U.S. And my mom Rosa now works in San Rafael.

My ancestors on my mother's side are also Filipinos. My grandma Amalia works in the U.S. post office in San Francisco. Her mother was a plain house wife and once a while helped with my grandma Amalia's Father with his business.

My ancestors in my Father's side are both Fillipinos, too. My grandma Teresita is a retired school teacher and is now liveing in L.A. Her parets were farmers. My grandpa Rogelio was a retired Regional Trial Court Judge and his parents had a huge farmland almost owned a whole town in the Philippins which was divided into portions where my Daddy inherited some.

When Marilou read her work in the author's chair, Orlando asked why her father died. "He had cancer," Marilou replied. Nai Hin said, "Your family owned a town? They must be rich!" Marilou shook her head. "That was long time ago," she said. "We don't own a town no more."

I complimented her on how much she had written about her ancestors. "My mom and grandma don't want to write," she said. "They tell me about their parents, and I write down what they say."

I was pleased that Marilou and her mother and grandmother had collaborated on this assignment, which had been a chief goal. I did not know how much of the actual writing was Marilou's, so from this piece I could not assess her writing ability. For that I would use her dialogue journal entries, which were written in class. But I had learned that Marilou had come from a line of farmers and professionals and that at one time her family had owned considerable land. We often forget that immigrants living in low-income areas or having menial jobs may in fact have received higher education and had professional careers in their own countries.

- "Ta Fou's Ancestors" (shown below) tells about this intermediate-level ESOL student's parents and his family roots in Laos. From Ta Fou's piece, I had no evidence that he had discussed the assignment with family members. But I did learn that his father was not living at home and that his family valued education. "How much money do your dad give you?" asked Nauyana. "Sometime 20 dollar," answered Ta Fou. The children seemed impressed. "Was the war bloody?" asked Ramon. When Ta Fou hesitated, I said that the war he was talking about is what Americans call the Vietnam War, but there was a war in Laos, too. It was indeed bloody. Horribly bloody. Many people had to leave their homes, and some of them came to America. "Lots of people die, my mom and dad say," said Ta Fou. "My daddy got shot right here," said Orlando, pointing at his chest. "On 11th Street." In the conversation that ensued, I found out that there had been violent deaths in seven of my students' families.

- I received four replies written in the hand of a parent. This may not appear extraordinary, but because this was my first attempt to get family members to write, I was pleased by any success. From these pieces I learned that some parents were willing to share with us aspects of their family histories. In a state known for its anti-immigration propositions, parents of color wrote with pride about their backgrounds. I was interested in the content of their writing, but I was also impressed by the parents' willingness to contribute and hoped that it was the prelude to a long collaboration. Jagjit's mother wrote about her elegant and heroic forebears in her native land, India. Notice, in the excerpt that follows, how proud she is of her heritage:

> My grandmother was polite and liked to help other people. Her parents were very rich. She came to visit us in a beautiful carriage . . . .

Ta Fou's Ancestors

My mother was born in Laos, my father is also born in Laos. My mother is a teacher at Lake's children center, my father have his own business, He does not live with me. He lives in Alaska. When my father comes to visit me, he would give me money. My ancestors fled to America because they have a war in their country. They came to America to study.

My grandfather was very respected in our village. He liked to give big donations . . . .

My mother was held captive by thieves and she was brave and escaped.

Cheng's mother, a Mien from Laos, wrote about how they had been forced, on account of the war, to flee to the United States. She came to California at an early age and considered it to be her homeland. From her writing, I could see how much she admired and loved her grandmother, and how the old stories of life in China and Laos were being kept alive:

Since my parents are not able to write in English, when I asked my parents about their parents, the answers I recieved from them was that both of my grandma and grandpa had very large families. Both my parents' parents grew up in China. My grandfather passed away during the war. My grandmother was living and was able to fled to United States. My grandmother is one of the oldest person in our family line to lived to the age of 89 years old. She was loved by so many families. My grandmother used to tell us stories of her years growing up in peaceful time of farm life. Before my grandmother passed away, she was a great-great grandmother. She lived a long and a contend life.

- At the fall parent-teacher conference, I asked parents if they had liked this assignment, and nearly all said that they had, an exception being one who did not know much about her ancestors. A mother laughed as she told me how her son had called his grandmother, her mother, and had found out things she had not known. Some said that they had not felt comfortable writing themselves because their English was not so good, but that they appreciated my interest and did not think I was prying. I remarked that I wanted to make home visits, and all appeared receptive, though one, a Mien mother, said she would have to ask her husband.

The following year, without changing the procedures, I received 12 parent responses. One reason for the increase may be that I had done this project twice before and parents, having heard by word of mouth about my desire for them to write, had gotten reassurances from other parents and were more willing to contribute. Another reason may be that our school's commitment to home visits had made parents more trusting of and positive about the parent-teacher relationship. A third reason may be that that year I happened to have 12 very responsive parents.

Names

The writing topic for the second week was *names*, which I selected because it (a) might reveal and celebrate cultural or family traditions, (b) might show the extent to which names (and possibly families) were becoming "Americanized," (c) was a first exploration into each child's sense of personal identity, and (d) would probably require a collaboration between the child and parents or other family members.

PROCEDURE

- The students and I brainstormed the subject, discussing why we had the names we did, what meanings names had, and what nicknames were.

- I told the students about my names and read them the letter I was sending to their parents. It included, "I was named James because that was my father's name. You might have given your child his/her name because you liked its sound."

- The students wrote their responses. Several of the responses showed that the children had discussed their names with their parents. For example, a beginning-level ESOL student, San Siew, wrote, "I ask why I have the name I do now Because I'm name after my Dad and what it means is that I'm the 3 son." A Mien instructional assistant told me that *San* means *third son* and that *Siew* is probably his father's middle name.

- "Maria's Names Project" (below) shows how the family of this nearly fluent speaker of English from El Salvador voted on which name to give her. I learned from Maria's piece that her family had a respect for democracy, that they were influenced by Lana Turner of U.S. movie fame, and that they had chosen a middle name for their child that was not Spanish. I asked Maria if she had known before this assignment how she had been named. She answered that she had known why she was named Lana but had not realized that someone had not wanted the name *Maria*.

Maria's Names Project

> My Name
>
> The reason they named me Maria was because my family had a vote. My family had Chosen three names. Three out of four of the people in my family picked Maria. My dad heard a actress named Lana and he liked the name.

Self-Portrait

The third writing project, a self-portrait, continued our exploration of each child's sense of identity and introduced a sophisticated literary device, the simile. It included an art project, so ESOL students, in particular, had an alternative to words to express themselves. This assignment gave the students a chance to celebrate their features or to make fun of them. As a self-portrait in similes, it was both them and not them, which gave the children freedom to take risks and play with language. ESOL students, who are more comfortable with literal expression, especially benefited from this structured opportunity to make up figurative language.

PROCEDURE

- We discussed in our class circle what a self-portrait was.

- At tables with access to a large class mirror, the children participated in the most familiar form of self-portraiture, drawing pictures of their faces with pastels. I gave no drawing lessons, but, noticing that several of the students were self-conscious over their efforts, I drew a self-portrait, demonstrating how to sketch. The children seemed encouraged—whether by my failure or my success, I am not sure.

- In the class circle, we discussed how we might describe our faces in words. Drawing on an idea from *Seeds Flying in a Fresh Light* (Fleming, 1988), a teacher resource book of activities for writing prose and poetry, I introduced the concept of *simile*. Together, we created a poem using similes to describe me, such as "My eyebrows are like bristles on a worn toothbrush."

- I suggested to the children that at home they use a mirror for this project. I also gave them a format for the poem:

    My hair is like . . .

    My eyes are like . . .

    My eyelashes are like . . .

    I included the poem that the class had written about me with the letter I sent home to parents and encouraged them to help their children.

- "Editha's Self-Portrait Poem" (on p. 44) was written by a beginning-level ESOL student with Filipino parents. Notice that she did not understand the function of the ellipsis points. When Editha read her poem in the author's chair, Juan said, "I like the way your teeth are like a cross-cutting saw." Melissa asked what she meant by "eyelashes like the hair of a horse." "The . . . you know," replied Editha, waving at her own neck. I asked, "What's that hair called that hangs along a horse's neck?" No one knew. "The mane," I finally told them. "The main what?" asked Juan. (Isn't English maddening?) Danielle's mother wrote a note to me about what a treat this assignment had been, which was the first such note I had ever received. I imagined Danielle with her mom, the two of them joking over the images they were creating.

- I displayed the poems on our hall bulletin board. Along with Editha's, I included the representational self-portrait she had done with pastels. Editha and the others were proud to show off their diverse features. Teachers appreciated that third graders were learning about similes, and the principal remarked, "The next step is metaphors. Just take out the *like*." Later I read

Home Work

1. My hair is like... a string.

2. My eyes are like... a big marble moving around.

3. My eyelashes are like... hair of a horse,

4. My eyebrows are like... my shoe brush,

5. My nose is like... a big bumb on the middle of the street,

6. My ears are like... a wig of a bird.

7. My cheeks are like... a big soft bed,

8. My mouth is like... a dark tunnel with voices in,

9. My lips are like... soft gelotine,

10. My teeth are like... cross cuting saw,

11. My tongue is like... a fresh meat.

12. My chim is like... a brown potato,

one of Editha's lines as a metaphor: "My mouth is a dark tunnel with voices inside." Might I be hearing her emerging voice? I could not be certain, for this had been homework. However, even if her poem had been a family collaboration of voices, I had accomplished one of my goals.

Treasures

The fourth week, I asked children to write about their favorite objects. I thought the topic would reveal aspects of the cultures in which they lived. For example, it might be an object that was produced by a traditional craft, or it might be a grandmother's necklace or a ring from the "old country."

PROCEDURE

- I told the students I wanted them to write about something that was very special to them. I said, "I'm thinking of some sort of object, not a pet. Give lots of detail."

- We brainstormed favorite objects, which I recorded on chart paper.

- In my own "homework," which I sent home to the parents, I wrote, "I own a wool, Irish sweater that is very special to me. I got it on a trip to Ireland, which is where some of my ancestors came from. It is a traditional fisherman's sweater with knitted designs. Except in hot weather, I wear it whenever I write stories. It's my writing sweater. After so many years, it has holes in it, but I love it just the same."

- The piece by Jeremy, a now-fluent former ESOL student, was typical—his favorite object was a Ken Griffey baseball jersey. That might tell us something about Jeremy's identity and reveal that he was an American boy, but it did not reveal his family history or Filipino culture. In fact, none of the responses produced anything close to what I had intended. I could only fault myself, however. Upon reflection, I realized that neither our brainstorming nor my sample made clear my interest in celebrating the students' backgrounds. My letter to the parents had not directly specified what I wanted. Indeed, it did not even ask for their children to write about traditional objects. I must have been hoping that by luck somebody would adore an object that had cultural, social, historical, or geographical resonance. Instead, I found that my students loved a soccer trophy, a "fake rabbit," a pencil box, a bike, the book *Aladdin*, a "Hello, Kitty" jewelry set, a Pocahontas doll, and a green coat. *Aladdin* was the favorite of a Filipino girl, whereas an African American girl loved Pocahontas. The children were careful not to pick pets; however, two of my students chose their little sisters as their favorite "objects"!

This final writing assignment was a failure in terms of my intended goals. I tried to remember one of our class maxims, "We like our mistakes because we can learn from them," and learn I did. I vowed that next time I would do the following:

- demonstrate more clearly the cultural significance of my "treasure," calling it, perhaps, an heirloom

- ask specifically for objects that tell about students' families, cultures, or histories

- request that the children be allowed to bring the traditional objects to school

- inquire about any stories the family can tell that relate to the objects.

The next year I made good on my vow, writing for the children and parents about an early 18th-century diary that had been passed down through the generations on my mother's side. The results were excellent. Most of the children brought in objects, and many of them were heirlooms. One of the more poignant ones was a pin with two stars. A Mien boy's great-grandfather had given it to his son, and he had worn it as a good luck charm all through the war. "My great-grandpa told him it was for his safety. I hope this stars can also bring me good luck someday." Other treasures included an 80-year-old quilt passed down through an African American family, an old photograph of ancestors in Mexico, a 63-year-old coin from India, and a bead bracelet made by a Mien

Anna's Treasures

> My grandpa gave my dad a silver nickles to my dad and my Dad gave it to me The end
>
> ^Dad's^
> My great geat grandma gave my great grandma a box whith some beat's and then my great grandma gave it to to my grandma and my grandma gave it to my dad and my dad gave it to me.
>
> Mom
> My great great grandma gave a tablocloth of a man holding a fork she gave it to my great grandma then my great grandma gave it to my grandma and my grandma gave it to my mom then my mom gave it to me to keep and reamber about my grandma at mexico.

grandmother. Anna brought three objects, two from her father and one from her mother. "Anna's Treasures" (above) tells of two family treasures that went back to great-great-grandmothers. I learned from Anna that her heirlooms had a purpose: to keep alive the memory of ancestors and the country from which they had come.

To be honest, not all reactions to this assignment were positive. At the fall parent-teacher conference, a mother confided to me that when her daughter had gone to her father to ask about a family heirloom, he had said, "Why they give this junk?" The mother explained that her husband had gone to school in Mexico, where the curriculum was very traditional: "They have textbooks and tests. That's all." The mother added that she and her husband came from broken families and that there was much bitterness and many severed ties. "It's not so good to talk about the old days," she said. I told her that, although I knew I was taking risks by asking questions about family and culture, I felt it offered, for the most part, a rich source of material for meaningful writing by the children.

Other Activities

Dialogue Journals

The students wrote for 20 minutes daily in their dialogue journals. I responded to each of them each day. The dialogue journals supported the unit in several ways. One was to improve the children's writing fluency. Another was to enable the students to experience writing as communication. Also, the dialogue journals gave them the opportunity to informally address the more formal writing assignments. Moreover, they helped build community, serving as a way for the children to learn about me and for me to learn about them. Finally, they were a means to assess on a regular basis how the students were progressing as writers.

> **Goal 3, Standard 1** To use English in socially and culturally appropriate ways: Students will use the appropriate language variety, register, and genre according to audience, purpose, and setting.
>
> ### Descriptor
> - determining appropriate topics for interaction
>
> ### Progress Indicator
> - interact through writing with an adult in a less formal setting

PROCEDURE

- When I introduced the journals, I asked the students to write from their hearts on any topic that inspired them. That afternoon I wrote responses to their entries. The next day, the students wrote replies to me before writing new entries. The students spent 20 minutes daily reading my responses, replying to me, and writing new entries.

- I illustrated "writing from the heart" by mimicking its opposite, a typical mall afternoon: "I went to the mall. I bought some stuff. I went home and went to sleep." I then recreated for the children how a former student had written about a dance she had performed:

    I was so excited! My whole family had come. I had practiced for hours and hours. Oh, what if I forgot the steps? I was so nervous! Then, just when I thought I was going to throw up, my turn came, and somebody pushed me onto the stage. I started dancing, and I could feel my family so proud and pulling for me, and I did great! I know because the audience clapped real loud and my dance teacher hugged me and my older brother didn't tease me.

- I also tried to respond "from the heart" to my students' writing. When I responded to the previous student, I commented on how proud I was of her:

You were nervous and scared, but you went on stage and danced anyway! That took courage! When I was your age, I would get nervous when I had to speak in front of the class. Even now I sometimes get scared if the audience is big. P.S. I love your writing!

- Sometimes I asked questions: "What kind of dance did you do?" I did not have time to write much because I thought it was important, especially at the beginning of the school year, to respond each day to everybody. I wanted the children to believe that nothing they wrote was unimportant.

- In her first entry, Nai Hin, an intermediate-level ESOL student whose primary language was Mien, wrote, "The thing I do at homoe is firs I went home and take a shower and when I'm dun with the shower I went out side and play with my friends and we play hi rope and jump rope!" I responded, "What is high rope, Nai Hin? Will you explain it to me?" She wrote back, "It is rubberband like you put it all to geter I'll bring one tomorw to let you see it so you could understand." This exchange illustrates the nuances of English and the misunderstandings that easily occur for second language learners. With the omission of an article in "What is high rope," I was asking Nai Hin to explain a game, but she thought I was asking her to describe the rope.

- Because I intended dialogue journals to stimulate fluency and voice, I did not correct them, though I did ask questions if poor spelling, limited vocabulary, or awkward structures interfered with our communication (e.g., I would write, "I don't understand. What is this word?"). However, I kept a record of each child's writing development, checking for topic, organization, clarity, sentence structure, spelling, mechanics (e.g., punctuation and capitalization), usage, descriptive words, and voice (by which I meant the writing's flow, power, and passion, that is, its capacity to engage a reader). I had time to assess each child about three times in that first month. A sample from Nai Hin's writing assessment log is shown on page 49.

- At least once a month, I conferred with each student. At my conference with Nai Hin, for example, I pointed out that she had written in standard English, "We play hi rope and jump rope!" But then she had misunderstood my question because "What is high rope?" does not mean the same as "What is *a* high rope?" If I noticed that several students had the same instructional needs (such as in the use of articles to clarify meaning), I taught a minilesson.

Language Arts Minilessons

A language arts minilesson is a short lesson on an aspect of standard English or the writing process. It involves direct instruction, generally to the whole class. During the first month of school, minilessons were prompted principally by dialogue journals and author's chair.

PROCEDURE

- Periodically, I reviewed the students' writing assessment logs and noted any patterns in their language usage. For instance, Nai Hin and many other children showed inconsistency in their use of end punctuation marks.

Nai Hin's Writing Assessment Log

NAME Nai Hin   DATES 8/7, 8/19, 8/25

ACTIVITY AND TOPIC:

8/7 Dialogue Journal: afterschool high rope.

8/19 Dialogue Journal: school and learning.

8/25 Dialogue Journal: day at beach.

⎫ Varies topic.

ORGANIZATION, SYNTAX, AND CLARITY:

8/7 Good sequencing. One long sentence made up of several sentences connected by "and."

8/19 Two sentences! Syntax prob.: "I like being in school is that to learn..." Clarity suffers. 8/25 Great sequencing. Shows logic and motive. Several sentences.

⎫ Learning sentences. Well organized clear.

SPELLING:

8/7 Compounds ("out side"). "Firs" (first), "dun" (done), "hi" (high).

8/19 "then" (than), "cheeting," "gards" (grades).

8/25 "bich" (beach), "tiyer" (tired), "relast" (relax), "towl."

⎫ Good speller. Spells as she hears it

CAPITALIZATION, PUNCTUATION, USAGE, AND GRAMMAR:

8/7 Inconsistent end punctuation marks. Uses exclamation points appropriately. Uses "go" instead of "went."

8/19 Forgot to capitalize only one new sentence. Inappropriate capitalizing of "S" (sloppy?). 8/25 Confuses past/present tense. 4 run-ons. (Needs instruction on tenses.)

⎫ As content becomes more complex, punctuation suffers.

DESCRIPTIVE WORDS, FIGURATIVE LANGUAGE, AND DETAIL:

8/7 Good detail: "shower," "hi rope." No descriptive words or fig. lang.

8/19 No detail except in response.

8/25 Best so far - detail and descrip. lang.: "hot," "sand," "cool," "towel."

⎫ Inconsistent but progressing.

VOICE:

8/7 Says what she does, not how she feels.

8/19 Passionate about not cheating. Wants good grades!

8/25 Excellent! I could feel that sunburn and cool, soothing water.

⎫ Emerging strongly.

Inconsistency and experimentation, it seemed to me, indicated that the students were ready to incorporate another element of standard English into their writing.

- Having chosen a topic, I gave a 20-minute minilesson. In the case of end punctuation marks, I modeled the use of the three used in the English language.

- During lessons on standard English, I emphasized the reason for conventions: Writing is communication. Following the conventions permits the writer to be understood by any reader of English, just as legible handwriting enables others to read written communications accurately.

Goal 2, Standard 2   **To use English to achieve academically in all content areas: Students will use English to obtain, process, construct, and provide subject matter information in spoken and written form.**

Descriptor

- understanding and producing technical vocabulary and text features according to content area

Progress Indicator

- revise and edit written assignments

- The students then practiced. For end punctuation marks, I selected anonymous sentences from student work or sentences pertaining to the unit we were exploring and asked the children to write the sentences in standard English. For example,

    Where is Laos_

    Laos is in Southeast Asia_

    How beautiful the mountains are_

- The minilesson on run-on sentences came about because Nai Hin did what many beginning writers do: She overused the conjunction *and.* I gave a minilesson in which I pointed out how much more powerful writing is if it is broken into sentences and does not go on endlessly in one incredibly long sentence. I challenged the students not to use *and* (unless appropriate) in their next dialogue journal entry. If they found they had used *and*s, they were to erase as many as possible. Several students kept asking me, "Is this *and* OK?" After this minilesson, some students (not all!) were more conscious in their writing of the use and misuse of conjunctions.

- Sometimes minilessons arose spontaneously, especially during author's chair. For example, if students were not paying attention to a reader, I stopped the reading and discussed with them the importance of listening. I also demonstrated how I listened to readers. I did not play with toys, talk to neighbors, or make faces at students. If I did, I would not hear the reading very well and I would be distracting others as well. I did *active listening:* I looked at the reader or down at the rug and focused all my listening power on what the reader was telling me. I also pointed out that readers could help their classmates listen by "performing" their piece. Here I demonstrated how boring a reading sounded when it was done softly and in a monotone, and then I repeated it, showing how it sounded if when it was performed dramatically, the words spoken clearly and audibly, with varying volume. I suggested that readers read as if they were giving us a very important message, which they were.

- For spelling and vocabulary support, we also developed a word wall upon which we placed alphabetically the words students were misspelling, new vocabulary they were learning during the unit, and spelling requests made during dialogue journal writing.

ASSESSMENT

I assessed the effectiveness of minilessons by monitoring the children's writing progress and by observing their behavior during author's chair and, later, during writers' workshop.

Conclusion

People of color, especially those living in poor neighborhoods, often perceive schools as White establishments, and many teachers and administrators are ignorant, even fearful, of "those people" and the neighborhoods in which they live. This unit, the impetus for which was my desire to get to know my students, turned into much more. It became a means by which I got to know families and could show that I valued their lives. Indeed, their histories, cultures, and countries of origin became a large part of my curriculum. Moreover, parents and children got to know me and became more comfortable with our school. The unit was foremost about building a community, largely through written communication, that included students, their families, and me.

There were other outcomes, all successful to varying degrees. The unit, coming at the beginning of the school year, cultivated a good learning environment. Through author's chair, we nurtured a community of creators and learners who took pride in their voices and listened respectfully to the contributions of others. Cooperation and collaboration were developed by means of community-building activities. Homework was meaningful, as it encouraged parent contributions, and children had opportunities to present their pieces in class and display them publicly. Writing was celebrated as communication, affirming that we had important things to say to one another and that we needed to be understood.

I realized I could not let this unit end. As Thanksgiving approached, I wondered what harvest celebrations were particular to the various cultures and what traditions each of my children's families maintained. Throughout the year, occasions arose that lent themselves to inquiries into my student's backgrounds and present lives.

"Who is your teacher?" I had asked that Mien child not so long ago. "You, Mr. Hughes! You!" Indeed, I was. But he was my teacher, too, was he not?

REFERENCES

Fleming, G. (1988). *Seeds flying in a fresh light: Activities to release the creative writing in students.* San Francisco: Author.

State of California. (1997). *Standards for the teaching profession.* Sacramento, CA: Author.

TESOL. (1997). *ESL standards for pre-K–12 students.* Alexandria, VA: Author.

Yarbrough, C. (1994). *Tamika and the wisdom rings.* New York: Random House.

UNIT 3
Facing Hardships: Jamestown and Colonial Life

DOROTHY TAYLOR

Introduction

Twelve small hands darted in and out of the Jamestown model, erecting the Popsicle-stick walls, gluing trees around the outside of the walls, and carefully placing cannons inside the walls. The hands belonged to my six fourth-grade ESOL students, who were assembling the various components that they had planned, designed, and constructed over the past week. The model of the fort at Jamestown was the culminating project of a 5-week unit on Jamestown and colonial life that had begun when the students visited the site of the fort with their mainstream classes.

In the fall, all of the fourth-grade classes in our school went on a field trip to Jamestown, Virginia, and the colonial village of Williamsburg. It was an ambitious project, a 3-day trip that required no small amount of planning and preparation. Although our school's other ESL teacher and I were unable to join the children on the trip, we were determined that our ESOL children would not miss this opportunity. Translators put informational papers into the children's native languages and made telephone calls to the children's homes, and we made sure that financial support for needy families was available. In the end, all but one of our ESOL children went on the trip. The parents of the child who did not go shared personal and religious reasons for their decision, which we felt compelled to respect.

The children returned from their trip eager to tell me what they had learned. "Can we make a fort like the one at Jamestown?" asked Heriberto. "Yeah, it so cool," José

Context

Grade level: Fourth grade

English proficiency level: Beginning

Native languages of students: Farsi, Japanese, Spanish, and others

Focus of instruction: ESL/social studies

Type of class: Pullout ESL, daily 1-hour classes

Length of unit: 5 weeks

chimed in. Yoko, who seldom talked, just grinned widely and nodded her head. Their excitement and eagerness about the subject fit right into my plans to incorporate a study of colonial life into our ESL class. The fourth-grade classes had chosen that particular field trip because the focus of their social studies curriculum was on Virginia history. This focus was connected to our school district's program of studies, which in turn was influenced by the state's newly implemented Standards of Learning (SOL; Commonwealth of Virginia Board of Education, 1995).

In addition to the personal interests of the students and the external curricular requirements of the school and the state, I felt that a study of Jamestown and colonial life would make a suitable academic and linguistic match for this particular group of students. Although the class was sumptuously small in number and all the students fell within the school system's categorization of beginning-level ESOL students, this group of six children presented a challenging range of language and educational backgrounds. The truest beginner was Yoko, who came from Japan at the beginning of the year speaking no English. She was, however, literate in her native language and was already starting to transfer those skills into English. José and Javier had arrived from Central America within the previous 2 years. Their spoken English was at an intermediate level, but their reading and writing skills were still at a low level. The remaining three students were children of immigrants. Born in the United States, their speaking approached nativelike fluency, although they continued to speak their native languages at home. They were included in the beginning-level class, however, because of their low reading and writing levels. Wilberto and Heriberto were diagnosed as learning disabled during the course of the school year. Mohammed, although born in the United States, had experienced interruptions in his education over long visits to his parents' native land, Iran. All of the children were reading two or more grades below grade level.

Unit Overview

I decided that a unit that addressed the hardships faced by the Jamestown colonists would allow my students to connect with their social studies curriculum. I also knew of many hands-on activities and readily available easy reading texts on the subject that would help this diverse band of linguistically and academically challenged children connect with the content. To these activities, I decided to add some explicit language practice in *wh-* questions. In observations of the students, particularly in their mainstream classes, I had noted that they were reluctant to ask questions or volunteer answers. Fact-based questions about people, places, and dates in Virginia history were also part of the recently implemented SOL in the state (Commonwealth of Virginia Board of Education, 1995), and I wanted to give my students the tools to address these requirements. Hence, my unit goals were as follows:

- improve reading skills, including phonics, word recognition, and comprehension of context clues
- increase English vocabulary about colonial America
- identify hardships faced by colonial Americans, particularly in Jamestown
- identify important people in U.S. history, particularly in Jamestown
- prepare the students to take the history and social sciences section of Virginia's SOL assessment (Commonwealth of Virginia Board of Education, 1995)

Our weekly lessons for this unit tended to follow a progression of what I thought of as information input, information output, and explicit language practice. During the information input activities, the students were sharing with each other what they knew about Jamestown and colonial America and acquiring additional knowledge and vocabulary by reading and, in the first week, watching a video. We read almost every day, but the emphasis at the beginning of the week was on acquiring language, so we spent more time then on reading activities. Toward the end of the week, we spent less time on reading as the students applied their knowledge in hands-on activities, such as making cornhusk dolls and drawing and labeling posters. I thought of these activities as information output. We spent about 30 minutes on Thursdays and Fridays on explicit language practice focusing on asking and answering *wh-* questions pertaining to the content we were studying and the students' personal lives. We devoted our final week to tying together the information as the students made a model of the Jamestown fort and wrote a

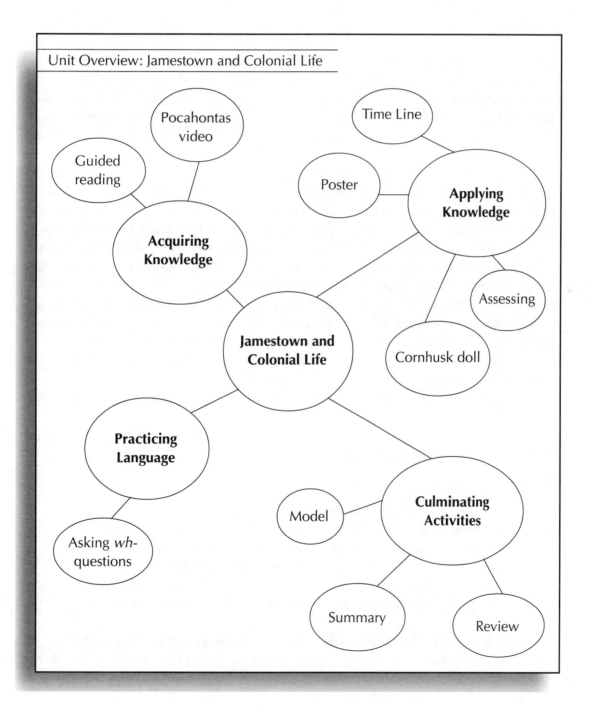

Unit Overview: Jamestown and Colonial Life

summary as a final project. During that week, the students also completed written review exercises from their textbook.

Because some of these weekly activities were ongoing and recurring, I decided to organize the activities that follow in a progressive sequence of *acquiring knowledge* (information input), *applying knowledge* (information output), *practicing language* (explicit language practice), and *culminating activities.* The unit overview on page 55 shows the activities in each part of the sequence. The 5-week lesson plan on page 57 shows how I organized these activities each week. This lesson plan includes a few ongoing activities not described in this unit: oral share, journal writing, and a spelling review. The oral share and journal writing gave the students an opportunity to talk and write on topics of their own choosing, and the spelling review prepared the students for the weekly spelling tests in their mainstream classes. I have not included these activities because they were not part of the Jamestown unit.

Standards

I began teaching in my school district 2 years ago, after a hiatus of 8 years in which I had worked with adult ESOL students. During that time, the need for educational standards and implementation of those standards had received unparalleled attention in the public schools. I found myself inundated with acronyms related to these standards as I struggled to learn how our school district's program of studies connected with the state's new SOL (Commonwealth of Virginia Board of Education, 1995). You might imagine that TESOL's addition of yet one more set of standards into the educational formula would have sent me over the edge. However, the opposite case is true. I found that *ESL Standards for Pre-K–12 Students* (TESOL, 1997) completed a much-needed piece of the educational whole and served to balance the standards addressed by other systems.

I included much of the content in our unit on Jamestown and colonial life to help my students meet the state's SOL. *ESL Standards* helped me recognize and address the particular needs of my ESOL students and understand that these standards are important to the ESOL child's success. Rather than adding to my planning burden, the standards, and particularly the descriptors and progress indicators within the standards, helped me develop activities and assessment tools that would address and meet the particular needs of my students. I planned my activities with both sets of standards in mind. Although the state standards often guided my choice of content, *ESL Standards* guided my way of addressing and measuring that content, especially in ways that were socially and culturally valuable.

Activities for Acquiring Knowledge

Modified Guided Reading

> The six children are seated around the table discussing the first chapter of
> Pocahontas *(Greene, 1988), which they have just read.*
> Javier: If I Pocahontas I shoot them strangers.
> Heriberto: How you gonna shoot 'em? She don't have no gun.
> José: [points to word brave *in text] Mrs. Taylor, it say here*
>   *Pocahontas say, "I will be . . . ." What that mean?*

All of the students in this group were reading 2 or more years below grade level, and one of my goals was to help them develop reading strategies that would help them become competent readers for their own pleasure and meet their academic needs.

Five-Week Lesson Plan

Jamestown and Colonial Life

	Monday	Tuesday	Wednesday	Thursday	Friday
Week 1 People in Jamestown *Who?*	Oral share (15 min.) Read *Pocahontas* (30 min.) Journal writing (15 min.)	Oral share (15 min.) Read *Pocahontas* (15 min.) Begin *Pocahontas* video (30 min.)	Oral share (15 min.) Read *Pocahontas* (15 min.) Continue *Pocahontas* video (30 min.)	Finish *Pocahontas* video (30 min.) Ask *who* questions about Jamestown (30 min.)	Oral share (15 min.) Ask *who* questions about selves (30 min.) Spelling (15 min.)
Week 2 Problems in Jamestown *Where?*	Oral share (15 min.) Read *Virginia History* (30 min.) Journal writing (15 min.)	Oral share (15 min.) Read *Virginia History* (30 min.) Begin posters (15 min.)	Oral share (15 min.) Read *Virginia History* (20 min.) Continue posters (25 min.)	Oral share (15 min.) Read *Virginia History* (20 min.) Ask *where* questions (25 min.)	Oral share (15 min.) Ask *where* questions about selves (30 min.) Spelling (15 min.)
Week 3 Products of Jamestown *What?*	Oral share (15 min.) Go over parts of corn (30 min.) Journal writing (15 min.)	Oral share (15 min.) Begin making cornhusk dolls (30 min.) Read *Corn Is Maize* (15 min.)	Oral share (15 min.) Read *Corn Is Maize* (15 min.) Finish making cornhusk dolls (30 min.)	Oral share (15 min.) Read *Corn Is Maize* (20 min.) Ask *what* questions about corn (25 min.)	Oral share (15 min.) Ask *what* questions about selves (30 min.) Spelling (15 min.)
Week 4 Events in Jamestown *When?*	Oral share (15 min.) Read *Virginia History* (30 min.) Journal writing (15 min.)	Oral share (15 min.) Read *Virginia History* (30 min.) Introduce time lines (15 min.)	Oral share (15 min.) Read *Virginia History* (15 min.) Finish time lines (30 min.)	Oral share (15 min.) Read *Virginia History* (20 min.) Ask *when* questions about Jamestown (25 min.)	Oral share (15 min.) Ask *when* questions about selves (30 min.) Spelling (15 min.)
Week 5 Review of Jamestown	Oral share (15 min.) Plan Jamestown fort (30 min.) Journal writing (15 min.)	Oral share (15 min.) Make Jamestown fort (45 min.)	Oral share (15 min.) Continue Jamestown fort (45 min.)	Oral share (15 min.) Write Jamestown summary (45 min.)	Oral share (15 min.) Review exercises on Jamestown (30 min.) Spelling (15 min.)

During the course of the 5-week unit, we read two books (*Pocahontas,* Greene, 1988; *Corn Is Maize,* Aliki, 1986) and a chapter in *Virginia History in Plain English* (Moran, 1998), written specifically for ESOL students by an ESL teacher in our school district. With each of the texts we read, I used a modified **guided reading** approach.

Goal 2, Standard 3 **To use English to achieve academically in all content areas: Students will use appropriate learning strategies to construct and apply academic knowledge.**

Descriptors

- focusing attention selectively
- applying basic reading comprehension skills such as skimming, scanning, previewing, and reviewing text
- actively connecting new information to information previously learned

Progress Indicators

- scan illustrations to make predictions
- skim chapter headings and bold print to determine the key points of a text
- verbalize relationships between new information and information previously learned in another setting

---

PROCEDURE

Although the focus on specific skills changed from day to day, the procedure for addressing a text was fairly consistent.

- I introduced the topic for the reading and the students shared what they knew about the subject. For example, before we read *Pocahontas,* I asked the children if they knew who she was. "She's a Indian," Wilberto said. "She saved that man, uh, what his name?" added José. "John Smith," shouted Heriberto, "and then she marry him." "No she didn't," corrected Wilberto, "she married John Rolfe."

- Our next step was to "walk through" the book, focusing first on the cover and then the inside illustrations. In the case of *Pocahontas,* the children were quite knowledgeable. They were able to identify the scenes and characters on the front cover and throughout the book. Occasionally I would ask Yoko, who was still in her silent period, to express her opinion by pointing to a person or object.

- As we looked through the book, we discussed key words for understanding

> Because many beginning-level ESOL children go through a silent period of up to 6 months, I encourage them to participate in class discussions by drawing or pointing to a picture. Rather than simply asking them to point to an object (e.g., "Point to the tree"), I prefer to ask their opinions ("Point to the man who you think is the chief.").

the text, and I wrote these words on the board, sometimes making a quick drawing so the students could look up and make the connection as they were reading. For example, in chapter 1 of *Pocahontas*, the words *stranger* and *strange* are used several times. I demonstrated with a picture of someone they knew and someone they did not know. I then taped the picture of the person the students did not know on the board next to the word *stranger*.

- After we had finished our walk-through, I asked a couple of questions about the content and elicited some opinions about what they had read to help them focus their reading. Our discussions on the topic before we looked at the book and during our walk-through guided my choice of questions. For example, I realized that the children already knew quite a bit about Pocahontas, so rather than ask explicit questions about who she was, I asked them why Pocahontas thought the new people were strange and how they would have felt if they had been Pocahontas.

- After I gave them their focus questions, the students scattered around the room to read the text independently for about 15 minutes. As they read, I asked individual students to read aloud to me for about 5 minutes each. Occasionally, when time was limited, I read the chapter to them.

- Back in the whole group, the students discussed their answers to my questions and raised questions about vocabulary or the text. I would often use this time to give minilessons on reading strategies (connecting letters with sounds, using pictures and context to predict word meanings, recognizing different punctuation marks). For example, as José and Javier read to me, they both stumbled over the word *thought*. As the students were returning to their table for the whole-group discussion, I wrote the words *thought, night,* and *light* on the board. I explained that the *gh* in these words is silent. The next day I challenged them to find the three words on page 13 of chapter 2 that had a silent *gh* (*highest, taught,* and *thought*).

ASSESSMENT

I kept a modified running record on each student.

- While each child was reading to me, I recorded observations in that student's record.

- Following each guided reading session, I noted any reading strategies, such as those that I mentioned above, that I needed to address in future lessons. Shown on page 60 are my notes on Javier's reading, which led to the lesson on the silent *gh*. In my records, I noted miscues, particularly patterns, such as missing *th* sounds and endings. I also recorded areas of strength. For example, I noted that Javier correctly read the word *must* two times after I pronounced it for him and correctly pronounced *strangers* and *Pocahontas*, two key words that I had written on the board. *M.L.* refers to the minilesson on silent *gh*.

Video: *Pocahontas*

> The children had just finished watching the video.
> Mohammad: Mrs. Taylor, I feel sorry for John Smith.
> Mrs. Taylor: Why do you feel sorry for him, Mohammad?

```
Sample Modified Running Record

NAME  Javier

BOOK  Pocahontas
```

Date, page no.	Miscues	Notes
11/18 p. 5	through — must - m— ended looked there —	no th must x √√ strangers √ Pocahontas √ miss'g ed's M.L. silent gh (11/18) (11/19)

Mohammad:	'Cause he almost died and he don't even get to get married with Pocahontas.
Javier:	Yeah, he do. He marry with Pocahontas and go to England. Don't you see that?
Mohammad:	No, he didn't. John Rolfe got married with Pocahontas, not John Smith. Right, Mrs. Taylor?

A couple of the students had seen Walt Disney Productions' animated video *Pocahontas* (Pentecost, Goldberg, & Gabriel, 1995) and made comparisons to the video as we read the book. When the students asked if we could watch the video in class, I was happy to comply. By watching the video, the students were able to verify pictorially what they had just read. It also helped them connect a face, albeit a cartoon one, to the names of important people in Jamestown.

Goal 1, Standard 2   To use English to communicate in social settings: Students will interact in, through, and with spoken and written English for personal expression and enjoyment.

Descriptor

- describing, reading about, or participating in a favorite activity

Progress Indicator

- watch and respond to a video

- The students watched the video, asking questions and making comments as they watched.

- Afterward, we discussed the students' favorite parts of the video and reviewed the characters.

ASSESSMENT

I noted that the children were completely engaged while watching the video. They often asked questions, which I used to clarify any misunderstandings. Their comments demonstrated that they were making connections with the text they had read. Follow-up activities in explicit language practice and reading response provided more formal assessments of the children's understanding of specific aspects of the content than watching the video did.

Activities for Applying Knowledge

For each of our readings, I planned an activity that would allow the students to respond to the text pictorially, graphically, or kinesthetically. As beginning-level speakers and readers of English, they needed a way to deepen and clarify their understanding of the text outside of or in conjunction with the realm of words that they were still developing. Activities gave them an opportunity to demonstrate that knowledge and gave me an opportunity to assess it. All of these response activities shared the following goal and standard, although each activity also met additional standards. Because the descriptors and progress indicators differ by activity, I describe the activities separately.

Goal 2, Standard 1   To use English to achieve academically in all content areas: Students will use English to interact in the classroom.

Descriptors
- following oral and written directions, implicit and explicit
- negotiating and managing interaction to accomplish tasks

Progress Indicators
- request supplies to complete an assignment
- ask a teacher to restate or simplify directions
- ask for assistance with a task
- negotiate turn taking to share supplies

Poster

The students are seated together looking at a chart and listing the problems that the settlers in Jamestown experienced in their first year.

Mrs. Taylor: You remember that one of the problems the settlers had was that the supply ship from England never came. Imagine that you're going to draw a picture to show that. What would you draw?

Wilberto:	I'd make the people looking sad.
Heriberto:	I'd draw the water and no boat.
José:	I'd draw the boat and then I'd do this [draws an X] to show it don't come.
Mrs. Taylor:	Those are great ideas. Let's draw one of them next to this sentence on the chart.

As we reviewed the section from the text on difficulties that the Jamestown colonists encountered, I noticed that the students were having trouble remembering the six problems outlined in the book. This activity was a way to help them focus on and more clearly understand those difficulties.

Goal 2, Standard 2 To use English to achieve academically in all content areas: Students will use English to obtain, process, construct, and provide subject matter information in spoken and written form.

Descriptors

- retelling information

- selecting, connecting, and explaining information

- representing information visually

Progress Indicators

- locate information appropriate to an assignment in text or reference materials

- read a story and represent the sequence of events through pictures and words

- edit and revise own written assignments

PROCEDURE

- I wrote the six problems on large chart paper and asked each student to visualize what that problem would look like. After they came up with some ideas, the children took turns drawing pictures next to each sentence on the chart.

- I gave the students a piece of poster paper and instructed them to fold it into fourths, to choose four of the six problems, and to represent one in each quadrant.

- After they had completed their pictures, I took down the large chart and asked them to write a sentence about each of their pictures on a piece of practice paper.

- After they had completed their sentences, a classmate checked them for correct spelling and punctuation.

- The students added their sentences to the posters, and we displayed them on a wall outside the classroom that was devoted to student work (see sample poster on p. 63).

Sample Poster of Colonists' Problems

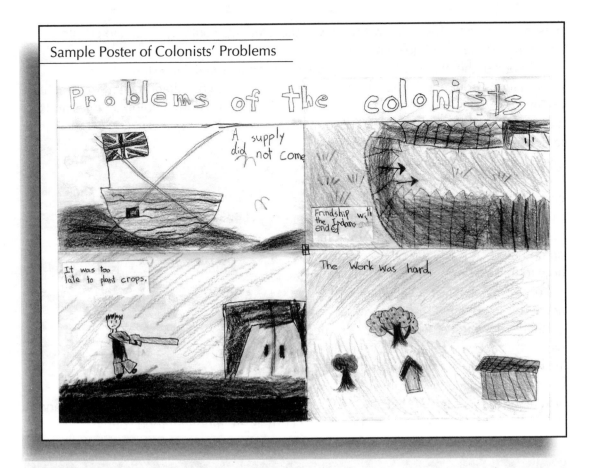

Cornhusk Dolls

> *The children are seated around the table following my instructions for tying a string around the top of the cornhusk to make the head of a cornhusk doll.*
>
> Mohammad: *Is this where you put the string [holding up his doll as I nod silently]?*
>
> Wilberto: *I think my head is gonna be too much big. [Mrs. Oto, a parent volunteer, shows him how he can move the string up to make the head smaller. She then moves over to Yoko, her daughter, who quietly asks her a question in Japanese.]*
>
> Mrs. Oto: *[to Yoko in English as she looks up to smile at me] Yes, string.*
>
> Mrs. Taylor: *Your buddy Heriberto can help you, José.*
>
> Heriberto: *[to José] You hold, I tie.*

The children in my class came from two mainstream classes. I met with my students' mainstream teachers at least once a week to plan activities for my class that would support the mainstream class instruction and to suggest ways to adjust the mainstream curriculum to meet the needs of ESOL students. During these meetings, I was able to share the ESL standards with the teacher and discuss ways to support these standards within the mainstream class. I also suggested that the teachers allow students to draw pictures to show what they had learned and encourage the students to ask for assistance in their native language from their same-language peers. Making the cornhusk dolls and presenting them to their class was one way that students could use realia to construct and demonstrate their knowledge of a subject.

In one of the mainstream classes, the teacher had asked each student to give a presentation about one aspect of life in colonial times. In consultation with that teacher, I planned a lesson on the study of corn as a crop produced during colonial times and as a means for making a colonial child's toy. These two topics fit into our Jamestown unit and into the options given by the mainstream teacher for presentations. Our study of these topics gave the students the support they needed to make a joint presentation in their mainstream class, one student presenting on corn as a crop and the other explaining how to make a cornhusk doll. It also gave Yoko, my non–English speaker, much-needed—and practical—oral practice. Yoko's mother, who volunteered in our class once a week, was able to translate any directions that Yoko was unable to follow in English. In the week that we made the cornhusk dolls, we also read *Corn Is Maize* (Aliki, 1986), which explains how corn is grown and used and describes how Native Americans developed corn as an important food source.

> Parent volunteers are valuable resources. Not only can they assist in instructional activities, but they can also serve as translators and adult role models for second language learning.

Goal 1, Standard 3   To use English to communicate in social settings: Students will use learning strategies to extend their communicative competence.

Descriptors

- focusing attention selectively
- seeking support and feedback from others
- comparing verbal and nonverbal cues
- using the primary language to ask for clarification

Progress Indicators

- ask someone the meaning of a word
- understand verbal directions by comparing them with nonverbal cues
- tell someone in the native language that a direction given in English was not understood
- associate realia with written labels to learn vocabulary or construct meaning

---

PROCEDURE

- I brought in an ear of corn, and we went over the vocabulary (*husk, ear, silk, kernels*). We discussed how the colonists grew corn and used the husks to make a child's toy.

- The students read a chart with step-by-step, illustrated directions for making a cornhusk doll.

- I modeled each step for the students, and they followed my actions to make the dolls. Mrs. Oto, our parent volunteer, walked around the class, helping students as needed.

- Two of the students used their dolls in their mainstream class presentation. The other students took theirs home to share with parents and siblings.

Time Line

> *Yoko and Javier are sitting at a table bent over Javier's sentence about events in Jamestown in 1612.*
>
> *Javier:* [*reading the sentence he has written*] *"The colonist plant mani tobako sed and sel the sed to England"*
>
> *Yoko:* [*pointing to the end of the sentence*] *You need period here.*
> [*Javier adds a period to the end of his sentence.*]
>
> *Yoko:* [*pointing to Javier's picture of a tobacco plant*] *What is this?*
>
> *Javier:* [*pretending to be smoking a cigarette*] *It's tobacco. You know.*
>
> *Yoko:* *Oh! Tobacco.* [*She opens her book and points to the picture and then to the word tobacco spelled correctly in the book.*]

In the third week of the unit, we finished reading the second section of the chapter on Jamestown in *Virginia History in Plain English* (Moran, 1998). This section reviews the problems that the colonists encountered and explains decisions and actions that took place in the colonies. The emphasis of this chapter is on the timing of these events. Knowing the dates of events in history is part of the state's SOL (Commonwealth of Virginia Board of Education, 1995). As a follow-up activity to our reading, we completed a time line exercise presented in the book.

Goal 2, Standard 2 **To use English to achieve academically in all content areas: Students will use English to obtain, process, construct, and provide subject matter information in spoken and written form.**

Descriptors

- writing about subject matter information
- selecting, connecting, and explaining information
- representing information graphically

Progress Indicators

- locate information appropriate to an assignment in text or reference materials
- construct a chart synthesizing information
- read a story and represent the sequence of events
- edit a peer's written assignment

PROCEDURE

- I demonstrated the idea of a time line by presenting one based on the unit we were studying. On the chalkboard, I drew a line with four dots labeled *1st Week*, *2nd Week*, *3rd Week*, and *4th Week*. I explained that we were making a time line and that each dot represented a week of our unit. Above the dot labeled *1st Week*, I wrote, "We learned about Pocahontas." I asked the students to tell me what we did the second, third, and fourth weeks and filled in the rest of the time line as they generated the information.

- After the students understood the concept of a time line, I explained that we were going to make a time line of the events in Jamestown. We reviewed the events in Jamestown included in the book. Then I placed a large time line with six dots on it in front of the class. The students took turns reading aloud the six important dates from their book as I wrote them under the six dots on the large time line.

> In this class, the number of students and sentences matched perfectly. When there are more students than sentences, I put students in pairs or small groups. I try to pair students in combinations that will complement their strengths (e.g., a fluent speaker/emergent writer with an emergent speaker/fluent writer or a good artist with a good writer).

- Each student chose one of the events to write about and illustrate. After they finished writing their sentences, they shared them with a student for peer editing.

- I looked over their sentences, did any final editing necessary, and then sent the students to fill in their information on the large time line at the front of the class.

> Students with learning disabilities often have difficulty copying text from the board. I give these students a smaller version of the text that they can use to copy in a quiet corner of the room where there are fewer distractions. The students can track the information they are copying more easily on the smaller piece of paper by using their finger or a bookmark.

- The students copied the information from the large time line onto the time lines in their study guides. They later used this information to study for the review exercises that they completed at the end of the unit.

Assessment

- I met regularly with students in reading and writing conferences. During conferences and after class, I made notes of students' progress and difficulties in oral language and writing in a notebook in which I kept anecdotal records. I used these notes when planning future lessons and activities. For example, when we worked on the hardship posters, I noted that Javier was the last person to complete his poster because he was easily distracted by the other students and wrote slowly and painstakingly. I gave him a pencil grip to help him write more easily. Also, for our next writing project, the time line, I paired him with Yoko, a more focused student who I suspected (correctly) would keep him on task.

Self-Assessment

Name _____

Date _____

Checklist for Making Cornhusk Dolls

	Never	Sometimes	Often	Comments
I followed directions.				
I asked questions when I didn't understand.				
I learned the words for making a cornhusk doll.				
I worked well with my buddy.				

Teacher comments:

- At the end of each application activity, the students completed a self-assessment checklist similar to one found in *Scenarios for ESL Standards-Based Assessment* (TESOL, in press). This checklist included progress indicators from the ESL standards. I collected the checklist, verified that it was accurate, and wrote comments containing noteworthy information, such as a student being particularly helpful to another student. I kept the checklists in a portfolio containing samples of the student's work, which I used in conferences with parents and mainstream teachers. A sample of the self-assessment for the cornhusk doll activity is shown above.

Activities for Practicing Language

Asking *wh-* Questions

The students are gathered around a game board playing the Who Game.

José: [rolling the dice] I got 3. I go 3. [He moves his marker ahead on the board three spaces and rests on a space with a large question mark.]

Mohammad: You gotta question. [He hands José a card with a large question mark.]

José: [reading the card] It say "King Jame I."

Mrs. Taylor: That's King James the First. [pointing to the I] Do you remember that that letter stands for the number 1 and means he was the first King James?

José:	*Oh yeah. Okay, Heriberto [who is sitting beside him].*
	Who is King James the First?
Mrs. Taylor:	*Good question, José. You can keep the King James*
	question card.
Heriberto:	*He's the king of America. [A couple of the children shake*
	their heads.] No, I mean, the king of England.
Mrs. Taylor:	*That's right! Javier, it's your turn next.*

On occasions when I had observed my ESOL students in their mainstream classes, I had noticed that they seldom asked questions or volunteered answers. Virginia's recently implemented SOL for history and social science includes a section on colonial life (see Commonwealth of Virginia Board of Education, 1995), and I realized that my students would be facing questions about important figures from colonial life and where and how they lived. I decided to include some explicit language practice in *wh-* questioning in our unit on Jamestown to prepare the students for this fact-based state test and to help them with questioning and answering skills that they could transfer to their mainstream classrooms.

Often, children grow quickly bored with explicit language drills but will happily practice a skill if it is incorporated into a game, so I decided to create the *wh*-question-word games. As I looked over my unit plans, each week's content seemed to converge neatly with the question words *who, where, what,* and *when.* Watching the video *Pocahontas* had helped the students connect faces to the important characters that they had been reading about. We played the Who Game in the first week, asking and answering questions about important people from the video. In the second week, our reading from the book on Virginia history provided a great deal of geographic information and prepared the students to play the Where Game, in which they asked questions such as "Where did the colonists come from?" and "Where is the James River?" In the third week, the students played the What Game by reviewing the materials we used to make cornhusk dolls and asking each other questions such as "What is the outside of corn called?" They played the When Game in the fourth week by asking questions based on the events on their time lines.

Goal 2, Standard 1   To use English to achieve academically in all content areas: Students will use English to interact in the classroom.

Descriptors

- asking and answering questions about content
- participating in a group activity
- negotiating and managing interaction to accomplish a task

Progress Indicators

- generate and ask questions on a specific subject
- formulate answers to a specific question
- take turns when playing a game

PROCEDURE

The students played a game in which they moved pieces around a game board to collect *who, what, where,* or *when* cards.

- I created the board by placing question marks and periods in spaces on a rectangular game board, which is shown below. I also made word cards that corresponded to the content under study that week; these cards had either a period (statement cards) or a question mark (question cards) under the words. Each week the question word *(who, what, where,* or *when)* changed. Answers were connected to the question word, as well as to the text we had read that week. However, as with guided reading, the procedure for playing the *wh-* game remained consistent from week to week.

- Prior to introducing the game, I gave a minilesson on correct word order in questions and statements. I wrote out "Who was John Smith?", putting each word and the question mark on a separate card. I placed the cards in random order on the table, and the children manipulated them until they were in the correct order. In this way, the children learned that the *wh-* question word goes at the beginning,

> *I like to give children cards to manipulate for grammar tasks such as this, which require precision and concentration. I find that it helps them focus, and watching how they arrange the cards gives me immediate feedback on the children's understanding of the task.*

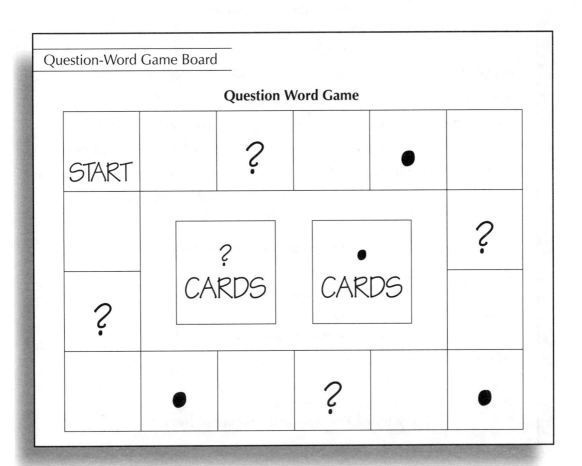

Question-Word Game Board

Question Word Game

followed by a verb, a person's name, and, finally, the question mark. After they practiced forming questions a few times, we followed the same procedure for statement order.

- The students took turns throwing the dice and moving ahead the number of spaces shown.

- If they landed on a question mark, they had to ask the person next to them a question beginning with the question word being practiced. For example, when we played the Who Game, a student who landed on a question mark picked up a question card. If *Pocahontas* was written on the card, the student whose turn it was would ask, "Who was Pocahontas?" If the question was correctly formed, that student kept the question card. If a student landed on a period, the person beside that student asked the question, and the student who chose the card had to form the correct answer (in grammar and content) to receive the statement card. A student who landed on a blank space did not have to do anything.

- Statement and question cards contained the same information, so if a student landed on a space with a period and drew the statement card with *Pocahontas* on it, the person beside that student would ask, "Who was Pocahontas?" (In this situation, no credit accrued to the person asking the

---

Content for Question-Word Game

Facts About Jamestown

Week 1 *Who?*	Week 2 *Where?*	Week 3 *What?*	Week 4 *When?*
John Smith	Jamestown	cornhusk	The Starving Time happened.
Pocahontas	James River	corn silk	Thomas Gates came.
Chief Powhatan	England	string	Lord de la Warr came.
John Rolfe	Virginia	head	Lord de La Warr got sick.
Christopher Newport	Atlantic Ocean	arms	John Rolfe got tobacco seeds.
King James I	London	ear of corn	John Rolfe married Pocahontas.

Sample Questions and Answers

Who?	Who was John Smith? John Smith was the leader of Jamestown.
Where?	Where was Jamestown? Jamestown was on the James River.
What?	[pointing to cornhusk] What is this? This is a cornhusk.
When?	When was the Starving Time? The Starving Time was in the winter of 1609.

question.) The student who drew the card would have to answer, "Pocahontas was the daughter of Chief Powhatan," or a similarly correct answer, in order to keep the *Pocahontas* statement card.

- Play continued until all the question cards and statement cards had been drawn. The student with the greatest number of cards was the winner. The question game content is shown on page 70, along with sample questions and answers.

ASSESSMENT

As stated previously, I noted any particular difficulties or progress in the students' anecdotal records. For example, Heriberto seemed to have consistent difficulty distinguishing the names of places, such as Virginia and England. After noting this difficulty in his records, I gave him a map of the area and asked him to label and color in the important places. We put this map in the front of the classroom for him to consult when we talked about the areas around Jamestown. Although he continued to give the wrong names for places on occasion, he now had a visual reference that he or I could point to in order to quickly clarify any misunderstandings.

For the most part, however, assessment for this activity was built into the rules of the game. By the time the students had completed the game by collecting a full set of question and statement cards, they had demonstrated the ability to successfully negotiate each of the progress indicators.

FOLLOW-UP ACTIVITY

The children loved playing the question-word game about Jamestown so much the first time that they initiated a follow-up activity:

Mohammad:	Mrs. Taylor, can we play the game again only with us?
Mrs. Taylor:	What do you mean, Mohammad?
Mohammad:	You know, we make card with us on it and ask questions.
Javier:	Oh, yeah. Like "Who is Javier?" "He is smart boy."
Mrs. Taylor:	Oh, so instead of cards with the names of people from Jamestown, you would make cards with your names on them and ask questions about each other?
Mohammad:	Yeah.
Mrs. Taylor:	[taking a stack of index cards from the desk and handing one to each student] That's a great idea. Why don't you each draw a picture of yourself and write your name on this card for homework, and we'll try it tomorrow?

The next day the children brought in their self-portrait cards. They used the same rules but asked *who* questions about each other instead of about people from Jamestown. I was delighted with Mohammad's modification of the game because it gave the children an important opportunity to interact socially and personally with each other. The children enjoyed this new version so much that I incorporated it into the following weeks' lessons. They continued to use their self-portrait questions, but in subsequent weeks asked each other *where, what,* and *when* questions, such as "Where do you live? "What do you like to eat?" and "When do you eat breakfast?"

Culminating Activities

Model of Jamestown

The students are examining the blueprint for the model of Jamestown and talking about the materials they will need to make their model.

Heriberto: *We're gonna need people. I got some little soldiers I can bring in.*

Wilberto: *We need walls for the fort.*

José: *I didn't see no walls there.*

Wilberto: *Yeah, they have walls [turns to page in textbook]. See. Like a triangle.*

Heriberto: *[looking at picture] Oh! I got some little trees I can bring, too.*

Throughout the unit, the students regularly reminded me that they wanted to make a model of the Jamestown fort that they had visited. I promised them that they could make one as their final project. Interestingly, Wilberto, who did not go on the field trip, was just as eager for this project. In fact, he had spent the time when the other children were on the trip scrutinizing his textbook and other books from the library on the subject. As the students planned and designed the fort, he corrected them and referred to his books so often that the students came to look on him as the class expert.

> **Goal 2, Standard 1** To use English to achieve academically in all content areas: Students will use English to interact in the classroom.
>
> ### Descriptors
> - requesting information and assistance
> - negotiating and managing interaction to accomplish tasks
> - expressing likes, dislikes and needs
>
> ### Progress Indicators
> - request supplies to complete an assignment
> - use polite forms to negotiate and reach consensus
> - negotiate verbally to identify roles in a class project
> - share classroom materials and work successfully with partners

PROCEDURE

- I suggested that the students make a blueprint of the model as a first step to help them organize not only the design of the fort but their roles and responsibilities for the plan as well. They drew a plan for the model on large chart paper spread out in front of them.

- They discussed the materials they would need to complete their model and listed them on another piece of chart paper. After they had completed the list of materials, they decided who would bring which materials and wrote the name of the person responsible on the materials chart. For example,

Heriberto had plastic trees and toy soldiers and would bring those, and Yoko had some small Native American figures to add.

- They divided the blueprint into sections, and individual students or pairs of students worked on different sections. Wilberto constructed the walls of the fort, José and Mohammad made cannons out of clay, and Yoko created the three ships in the harbor out of walnut shells.

- As the students completed items, they glued them onto a large piece of cardboard, using the blueprint to help them decide where to place the items. The students' eyes moved constantly back and forth from the fort to the charts as they consulted their blueprints.

This activity was designed and implemented by the students. My job was one of advisor and facilitator. I volunteered materials they needed, such as paper and modeling clay, and provided technical advice, such as how to make little ships out of walnut shells and how to find a picture of the British flag on the Internet.

- When the model was complete, we placed it in the school library (see below).

ASSESSMENT

I used the same assessment methods for this activity that I used for the application activities.

- I noted observations in the student's anecdotal records. For example, I noted the leadership role that Heriberto took in planning the fort,

Model of Jamestown Fort

Photo: Dorothy Taylor

```
┌──────────────────────────────────────────────────────────────┐
│  Sample Anecdotal Record                                       │
│  ─────────────────────────                                     │
│                                                                │
│    Student Name  Wilberto                                      │
│  ┌──────────┬───────────────────────────────────────────────┐ │
│  │   Date   │                   Notes                        │ │
│  ├──────────┼───────────────────────────────────────────────┤ │
│  │  12/10   │  Today as stds. were planning                  │ │
│  │          │  Jamestown fort, W. told J. that               │ │
│  │          │  walls of fort should be in                    │ │
│  │          │  triangle w/ gardens outside walls.            │ │
│  │          │  He flipped quickly to correct p.              │ │
│  │          │  in textbk. to prove his point.                │ │
│  └──────────┴───────────────────────────────────────────────┘ │
└──────────────────────────────────────────────────────────────┘
```

identifying materials we would need, and volunteering to bring in many of these materials. I also made a note of Wilberto's knowledge about details of the fort (see the sample anecdotal record shown above).

- In addition to my anecdotal records, the students completed a self-assessment checklist identical to the "Self-Assessment for Group Participation" included in *Scenarios for ESL Standards-Based Assessment* (TESOL, in press).

Written Summary

The students are sitting at the table with the completed Jamestown fort in front of them. I am sitting at the table, too, with a stack of paper strips in front of me. We are preparing to write a summary about the Jamestown settlement to add to the model.

Mrs. Taylor:	When we write a summary, we put in the most important information. What do you want to tell the people who look at your model about Jamestown? [As the students speak, I write the sentences on the strips of paper, correcting any grammatical errors.]
Yoko:	There is three ships. The Susan Constant, the Godspeed, and the Discovery.
José:	The settlers, they have many problems.
Javier:	Many of the peoples die cause they don't got no food.
Mohammad:	They builded the fort at the James River.
Wilberto:	The leader was John Smith.
Heriberto:	They come to get gold.

When I suggested to the students that we place their model of Jamestown in the library so it could enjoy a wider audience, they decided that they should include a written report to go with it. They wanted to make sure that students who saw the model would understand what it was and what had happened there.

> **Goal 2, Standard 2** To use English to achieve academically in all content areas: Students will use English to obtain, process, construct, and provide subject matter in spoken and written form.

Descriptors

- retelling information
- selecting, connecting, and explaining information

Progress Indicators

- write a summary of information in a book and/or video
- organize sentences into a logical sequence

PROCEDURE

- The students talked about what they considered to be important facts about Jamestown. As the students each told me at least one fact they would like to include, I wrote it on paper sentence strips that could be manipulated. Working together, the students put the strips into a logical sequential order.

- I placed the strips in the correct order on the board. I solicited a few more details and added that information to the sentences. I also guided the students to include an introduction and a conclusion, which I added to the sentences. I asked them to show me where the paragraphs should begin and end.

- When we had completed all of these steps, the children read the information to me as I wrote the entire report on a large piece of chart paper.

- The students copied this report into their journals, and Yoko word processed the report during writing lab.

- I made copies of Yoko's word-processed summary. The other students checked it against their journal copies and showed Yoko where her typing errors were. I assigned Heriberto to help Yoko locate the errors as she made the corrections on the computer.

- We attached Yoko's final draft to the model of Jamestown that was placed in the library.

ASSESSMENT

The writing activity was included in the self-assessment checklist that the students completed after finishing the Jamestown model. The students also completed a separate editing checklist after writing in their journals.

I used this information to plan future minilessons during writing workshop. For example, many of the students did not capitalize nouns, such as *James River* and *John Smith,* when they copied the report. In a later writing workshop, I explained the importance of capitalizing names of places and people, and used some names from Jamestown as examples.

Review Exercises

In most of the activities for this unit, the students participated as a group or in pairs. These activities allowed the students to support each other and develop much-needed social and verbal interaction skills. I used writing and reading conference times to assess and address individual students' needs. However, I also wanted to prepare the students for the kinds of paper-and-pencil tests they would need to take in the classroom and in standardized testing situations. In addition, individual assessments written by the students gave me concrete evidence of progress to share with mainstream teachers, other support specialists, and administrators. I used two review exercises at the end of the chapter on Jamestown in *Virginia History in Plain English* (Moran, 1998) to assess students individually. In one exercise, the students gave short answers to questions, and in the other they matched pictures to key vocabulary.

Goal 2, Standard 2   **To use English to achieve academically in all content areas: Students will use English to obtain, process, construct, and provide subject matter in spoken and written form.**

Descriptors

- understanding and producing vocabulary and text features according to content area
- selecting, connecting, and explaining information
- interpreting information presented visually

Progress Indicators

- identify people and places within a specific context
- write short answers to questions
- match pictures to key vocabulary

PROCEDURE

- The students worked individually to complete the exercises.
- After completing the short-answer section, they read their answers to me aloud. As they read, I added standard spelling above any words I was not able to read because of their nonstandard spelling. Javier's completed review exercise (from Moran, 1998, pp. 78–81) is shown on pages 77–79. Although many of his answers were difficult to read because of his nonstandard spelling, it was obvious as he read his answers to me that he understood the facts and concepts being assessed.

In my reading and writing records, I highlight any observations that suggest possible learning disabilities, such as letter reversals, and try to make careful notes about the circumstances surrounding the observations. I find these notes helpful in conferences with special education specialists or during pupil placement meetings.

Review

✓ 1. After Queen Elizabeth died, who became King of England? _James King_

✓ 2. Why did King James I want to build a colony in Virginia? _to Find gold_

_____

✓ 3. What were the names of the three ships that set sail for Virginia in 1606? _The Discovery_
✓ _constant_
The god Speed Susan
C

✓ 4. Who was Christopher Newport? _The_
ships
captain the three

78   **The Jamestown Settlement of Virginia**   **Chapter 4.1**

continued on p. 78

✓

5. Why did the Settlers name a river The James River, and their colony Jamestown? _James king_

_____

✓

6. Name 6 problems the settlers had at Jamestown:

Powhatans
1. pahtns, and.

mosquitoes   disease
2. mceos and Dses

have good   farmers
3. They no hv guo Foms

scared
4. They was Srars

meat
5. They no hv met

6. They wast to go
ao to get met

Chapter 4.1   The Jamestown Settlement of Virginia   79

continued on p. 79

ASSESSMENT

I gave the students a grade based on the accuracy of their answers. All of the students completed the test with at least 70% accuracy. I used this information, along with checklists, rubrics, and anecdotal records, to assign the students their ESL grades. I also shared the information with their mainstream teachers, who used it to help assign the students' social studies grades.

7. Who was John Smith? <u>John Smith</u>

became . leader
<u>BCM The Ler</u>

8. Who was Pocahontas? <u>pocahontas</u>

daughter of Powhatans
<u>was The Dr av pahths.</u>

Draw a line from the picture to its name:

1.

Susan Constant
Godspeed
Discovery

2.

The James River

3.

Jamestown

4.

John Smith

5.

Pocahontas

Final Assessment

The formal and informal information that I gathered during the unit often influenced the direction of my lessons within the unit. However, at the conclusion of this unit on Jamestown, I used my assessment material to conduct a more thorough evaluation. I assembled all of the assessment tools that I had used: self-assessment checklists, anecdotal records, running records, and the final written review exercises. I evaluated the data to see how well the students had met the general unit goals and the ESL standards (TESOL, 1997). I used these data to assign grades to the students and shared the data with the students' mainstream teachers and parents during conferences.

Many parents and mainstream teachers of ESOL students are concerned about how to appropriately evaluate and assess the abilities of these children, particularly when they are at a beginning level. Yoko's mainstream teacher and her parents had expressed these kinds of concerns to me. At this stage, Yoko was a silent learner. Her parents worked hard at home to help her, translating social studies and science texts for her and helping her complete written assignments. However, they were not native speakers and sometimes had difficulty understanding the texts themselves. In addition, Yoko's teacher felt he had no measure of how much of the work was Yoko's own. On the other hand, although still fairly quiet in my pullout ESL class, Yoko did occasionally speak, especially when she was asked a specific question. My reading records documented the fact that she was decoding with facility and understanding most of what she was decoding. However, it was in our hands-on activities, such as making the poster and cornhusk doll, that Yoko really exhibited her understanding and creativity. Her illustrations on the poster were rich in details, and when she made her cornhusk doll she gave him traditional Powhatan clothing and placed a bow in his hand with a quiver and arrows on his back. The samples that I collected of her writing were equally meticulous. When she was completing the review exercise, I assisted her by reading a few difficult words; she then answered all of the questions correctly.

When I invited Yoko's mother to volunteer in our classroom, she was reassured to see Yoko participating so fully. My anecdotal records, samples of hands-on activities, and written work convinced Yoko's mainstream teacher that she understood the content. In addition, these records and checklists that included the progress indicators from the ESL standards showed Yoko's teacher and our administrators that Yoko was meeting a set of ESL standards as well.

I used my assessment materials to evaluate students and to help me decide what to teach in reading and writing conferences with individual students. For example, my reading records showed that Javier was having difficulty with consonant blends, so we worked on these blends in reading conferences. In addition, during my review of the data, I looked for patterns of gaps or progress to help me plan areas to focus on with the group as a whole.

In anecdotal records from writing conferences and on the students' written test, I noticed that the students had expanded their vocabularies and were writing more complex structures, but their use of nonstandard spelling and lack of punctuation made some sentences unclear. I made plans to incorporate writing lessons and activities to address these issues in future lessons. I also noted that I had not addressed any of the standards included in Goal 3 of the ESL standards (To use English in socially and culturally appropriate ways: Students will use the appropriate language variety, register, and genre according to audience, purpose and setting; TESOL, 1997). I was not overly concerned about this observation because I was aware that many social and cultural standards had been addressed on their class field trip to Jamestown and in earlier units in our class.

However, I made a note to include in our next unit activities, such as drama or role playing, that would address these sociocultural standards.

Conclusion

This unit on Jamestown was one of the most enjoyable units I had taught because the students were excited and motivated throughout. Also, their enthusiasm after visiting Jamestown had a profound impact on the direction of the unit, which I had already been planning. For example, the model of the fort was completely their idea and became a very important means for me to assess their learning.

I was very fortunate to have such a small group of children because they had a variety of needs and came from a wide range of educational backgrounds. Although I occasionally made special adaptations to meet these needs, such as allowing the learning-disabled students to copy work separately and partnering fluent speakers with emergent speakers, I tried to build most of the accommodations for these special needs into the lessons themselves. Because the class was small, the students were able to apply their knowledge through hands-on activities that allowed for a wide range of abilities. During the guided reading time, I was able to listen to each child and help each one with any special problems, such as word reversals or difficulty connecting sounds and symbols. Perhaps one of the most important benefits of this small-group instruction was the collaboration and sense of community that the students developed. They learned to support and accommodate each other: Yoko helped Javier with his spelling, Heriberto translated the instructions for making the cornhusk doll for José, and José used his adept motor skills to help Heriberto tie the string around the arms of his doll.

RESOURCES AND REFERENCES

Aliki. (1986). *Corn is maize*. New York: HarperTrophy.
   This book offers a simple description of how corn was discovered and used by the Indians, and how corn is grown and used today. It offers a great combination of the history and science of corn and includes colorful illustrations by the author.

Bennett, C. T. (Sr. Consultant). (1991). *Virginia: The world around us*. New York: Macmillan/ McGraw-Hill School Division.
   This is the state history textbook many students in Virginia, including ESOL students, read in mainstream classrooms.

Commonwealth of Virginia Board of Education. (1995). *Standards of learning for Virginia public schools*. Richmond, VA: Author.

Greene, C. (1988). *Pocahontas: Daughter of a chief*. Danbury, CT: Children's Press.
   This book is an easy-to-read biography of Pocahontas and has many illustrations.

Moran, T. (1998). *Virginia history in plain English, Part 1*. Fairfax, VA: Benchmark Books.
   This study guide was written by an ESL teacher for the Fairfax County Public Schools. The simplified text and illustrations accompany the Virginia history text and curriculum.

Pentecost, J. (Producer), Goldberg, E., & Gabriel, M. (Directors). (1995). *Pocahontas* [Video]. Burbank, CA: Walt Disney Home Entertainment. (Available from Buena Vista Home Video, Department CS, Burbank, CA 91521)
   Disney's popular video about Pocahontas offers an animated version of Pocahontas' life. It is appealing to children because of its humor and catchy tunes.

TESOL. (1997). *ESL standards for pre-K–12 students*. Alexandria, VA: Author.

TESOL. (in press). *Scenarios for ESL standards-based assessment*. Alexandria, VA: Author.

UNIT 4
The Underground Railroad

SUE DEFABBIA

Introduction

> *You find the Big Dipper—go ahead 3 spaces.*
> *A wild animal bites you—go back 3 spaces.*
> *You eat good berries—go ahead 3 spaces.*
> *You arrive at a "station"—take 2 extra turns.*
> *You get caught by slave catchers—go back to start.*

These are some of the squares one might land on while playing Escape on the Underground Railroad, a game created by my third- and fourth-grade ESOL students in Rochester, New York. Through the process of making this board game, these students demonstrated and reinforced their learning about the challenges and triumphs experienced by thousands of slaves as they risked their lives following the North Star to freedom.

Unit Overview

The game described above was the culminating activity of a 6-week unit on the Underground Railroad. It was timed to correspond with Black History Month and coincided with our school's Genesee River Valley Project curriculum, which focuses on local environment and history as a backdrop for learning. Rochester was an important stop on

---

Context

Grade level: Third and fourth grades

English proficiency level: Intermediate to advanced oral skills; struggling as readers

Native languages of students: Lao, Spanish, Vietnamese

Focus of instruction: ESL/social studies

Type of class: Pullout, 40 minutes, 4 days a week, six students

Length of unit: 6 weeks

the Underground Railroad and for a time was also home to abolitionist and "conductor" Frederick Douglass.

The overall goals of this unit were to

- make the abstract concept of the Underground Railroad concrete for young learners
- develop a basic understanding of how the Underground Railroad operated and why it was necessary and important
- foster the development of higher order thinking skills
- have students use books to find information
- have students create a finished product that would clearly demonstrate learning and that could be shared easily with classmates and families
- build classroom cohesion through an enjoyable, cooperative, whole-group effort

My school is an inner-city neighborhood school with roughly 680 students in Grades K–6. We have a relatively small ESOL population, approximately 35 students served by a teacher working 80% of a full schedule. Most of our children live in poverty, with 93% receiving free or reduced lunch. There is a very high transience rate: About 40% of our district's student population moves from one school to another each year. Of the six students who participated in this Underground Railroad unit, only four had started the year with me. By the following year, three of the six students had moved on to other city schools.

This unit continued from a previous one about Dr. Martin Luther King, Jr., and slavery. I believe it is helpful for my students to have solid background knowledge of these issues, as I find that some of our ESOL families are fearful of or biased against the many African American families in their neighborhood. Through developmentally appropriate, in-depth exploration of the history and current issues surrounding race relations in the United States, I hoped my students would gain some insight into and understanding of the difficulties and complexities of the lives of many African Americans.

This particular group of students challenged my teaching skills more than any other all year long. Ricardo, Duong, and Kham were rather immature and somewhat disruptive (especially Ricardo). Elizabeth presented herself as mute when she entered our school in January—that is, until her cousin Amanda joined the class. Then they never stopped talking and giggling. Ngan was my one compliant student. The class met during the last 40 minutes of the day, when students in the mainstream classrooms were sweeping the floors and getting ready to go home. We were all tired! The afternoon announcements interrupted class every day. I dreaded this class and felt we desperately needed to do something engaging that would change the group's dynamic. The Underground Railroad unit, with its emphasis on the final, whole-group game-making project, transformed this class. It also provided rich opportunities for much language use, discussion, skills development, creativity, development of higher order thinking skills, and demonstration of knowledge. The unit overview (on p. 85) shows the unit activities.

I must mention, too, that this was my first year of teaching. I was more than a bit overwhelmed with all that that entailed. There was so much to figure out, not the least of which was how to present interesting, creative units that engaged my students and provided real opportunities for learning while maintaining order and my own sanity. As usually happens, while my students learned a great deal from this unit, I also learned a lot from teaching it.

Unit Overview: The Underground Railroad

Learning About the Underground Railroad

- Group read-aloud and discussion
  — Reading strategies minilesson
- Vocabulary development
  — Identification of words
  — Use of context; dictionary games
- Summarizing and questioning
- Written assessment
  — Answering questions minilesson
- Independent reading and writing
  — Sharing
  — Minilesson on good listening
- Picture book read-aloud
- What we learned

K-W-L Chart

- Define terms
- What do we know?
- What do we want to learn?

Underground Railroad Unit

Learning About Games

- What makes a good game?
- Play games
- Analyze games
  — Define terms

Sharing Feelings and Sharing the Game

- Write and share essays
- Ask permission of teachers
- Teach game to and play game with classmates
- Share with families

Making Our Game

- Brainstorming
- Creating list
  — List minilesson
- Writing and drawing
- Sharing, discussing, negotiating
- Writing instructions
  — Instructions minilesson
- Playing, editing, revising

Teacher's Plan Book

Monday	Tuesday	Thursday	Friday
Week 1: K-W-L; Group read aloud and discussion; vocabulary development; summarizing and questioning; written assessment			
K-W-L chart: Define terms and complete chart	. . . *If You Traveled* . . . : Read and discuss intro and chapter 1 (20 min.) Identify unfamiliar vocabulary (15 min.) "Reading strategies" minilesson (5 min.)	Vocabulary game (10 min.) . . . *If You Traveled* . . . : Read and discuss "What did it mean to be a slave?" (10 min.) Identify unfamiliar vocabulary (5 min.) Summarizing and questioning (15 min.)	Vocabulary game (5 min.) . . . *If You Traveled* . . . : Review and complete reading (10 min.) "Answering questions" minilesson (5 min.) Written assessment (20 min.)
Week 2: Independent reading and writing			
Vocabulary game (10 min.) Choose topics and read independently	Vocabulary game (5 min.) Begin writing first draft	Editing and rewriting	Vocabulary game (10 min.) "Good listening" minilesson (5 min.) Sharing circle (25 min.)
Week 3: Picture book read-aloud; what we learned			
Introduce *Barefoot*: Predict; read and pose questions	Vocabulary game (5 min.) Reread *Barefoot* and study illustrations	List of things learned: Model; work in pairs	Vocabulary game (10 min.) Group compilation of things learned
Week 4: Learning about games			
List of familiar games (5 min.) What makes a good game? (10 min.) Learn and play *Candyland* (25 min.)	Replay *Candyland* (10 min.) Question sheet review and whole group completion (30 min.)	Learn and play *The Secret Door* (15 min.) Complete questions in pairs (15 min.) Review with whole group (10 min.)	Learn and play *Hangman* (15 min.) Complete questions independently (15 min.) Review with whole group (10 min.)

continued on p. 87

Teacher's Plan Book, *continued*

Monday	Tuesday	Thursday	Friday
Week 5: Making our game			
Brainstorm about game	List minilesson (5 min.) Pairs: Create list of good and bad things	Vocabulary game (5 min.) Group 1: Writing language for game Group 2: Draw game (30 min.) Share and discuss (5 min.)	Continue two groups and sharing
Week 6: Making our game; sharing feelings			
Whole group: Drawing, writing, decorating, etc.	Whole group: Complete game (15 min.) Writing instructions minilesson (10 min.) Write instructions (15 min.)	Finalize game (5 min.) Play game (15 min.) Edit (10 min.) Replay (10 min.)	Play game (10 min.) Write and share essays (30 min.)
Weeks 7 and 8: Sharing the game with classrooms and families			

My revised teacher's plan book for this period shows what this 6-week, 4-day-a-week unit looked like on a day-to-day basis (see pp. 86–87). Each block lists major activities for that day. Each class period lasted 40 minutes.

Standards

In New York State, as in many areas of the country, new, higher learning standards are being adopted for all students (The University of the State of New York, State Education Department, 1996). Because the state recently began testing according to these standards, teachers are finding the expectations to be quite a stretch for many students, especially those in urban and poor districts such as mine. ESOL students are particularly challenged by language standards that many native speakers are struggling to meet.

Although the wording and format of the New York State standards are somewhat different from those in *ESL Standards for Pre-K–12 Students* (TESOL, 1997), much of the content and intent is similar. Both sets of standards emphasize the proficient use of the English language for academic learning, expression of ideas, and social communication and understanding.

I have found that using the New York State standards and sample performance indicators has helped me stay focused on what my students need to be able to do and accomplish to be successful in school (and, perhaps, in life). I make an effort to keep them in mind as much as possible throughout a unit and during the year. I do not necessarily think about the standards and then plan my units and lessons, but they are constantly in the background of my thinking, especially as I plan particular activities.

TESOL's ESL standards, with their very strong emphasis on the development of effective and appropriate social language use, also provide me with a clear mandate for assisting students with this crucial aspect of language acquisition. In the Underground Railroad unit, I was careful to provide many opportunities for students to relate to each other in pairs, through whole-group work, and in making presentations to their peers.

As a new teacher, I find that both sets of standards provide helpful frameworks within which to think about what I do in the classroom, and how and why I do it. One of my goals for improving my teaching is to be more overt in my use of the standards when planning. Another is to develop an effective method for combining the New York State and TESOL standards into one workable tool that I can use to plan my units and lessons.

Introductory Activity

K-W-L Chart

I often use a K-W-L chart to begin units. I find it a very effective technique for jump-starting students' thinking and interest in a topic. The first column, labeled *K* for *what we know,* gives me a tremendous amount of information about students' prior knowledge and the depth of their understanding on a topic, as well as where there are gaps or misconceptions. The *W*, or *what we want to learn,* section provides helpful insight into the students' interests. From this information, I am better able to plan my lessons and decide which areas will receive greater focus and attention. The last column, *L*, for *what we learned*, is usually not completed until near the end of a unit. This section is a useful tool for assessment and review. In this Underground Railroad unit, I never formally returned to the K-W-L chart. I felt it was unnecessary and would be somewhat redundant because the final project provided ample opportunities for the students to articulate their learning.

Goal 2, Standard 2 **To use English to achieve academically in all content areas: Students will use English to obtain, process, construct, and provide subject matter information in spoken and written form.**

Descriptors

- gathering information orally and in writing
- hypothesizing and predicting
- formulating and asking questions

Progress Indicators

- identify and associate written symbols with words
- generate and ask questions

PROCEDURE

- I told the class we would be studying the Underground Railroad as a follow-up to our learning about slavery and Frederick Douglass. I drew a blank K-W-L chart on chart paper and asked them to identify what the letters stood for. The students were somewhat familiar with this graphic organizer, so, after some prompting, they successfully defined the terms for the chart.

- I asked the students as a group to help fill in the first column by telling what they already knew about the Underground Railroad. "A train?" asked Amanda. "It go in a tunnel under the earth?" guessed Kham. It quickly became apparent that not one of these children had any idea what the Underground Railroad might be. After I provided several clues, they were still unsure, so we left the *K* column blank and filled in the *W* column with only the most basic questions: "What is the Underground Railroad?" and "Why is it important?"

At other times when I have done K-W-L charts with students, I have been amazed at how much they already knew. In this case, the opposite was true. Although we had spent part of a week learning about Frederick Douglass and they had studied Harriet Tubman in their mainstream classrooms, they had no idea what I was talking about, showing me that I needed to start at the very beginning. I also became aware that the Underground Railroad is a rather abstract concept for third and fourth graders. It took some effort to move beyond this literal image.

Activities for Learning About the Underground Railroad

We spent the following 3 weeks doing a variety of reading and writing tasks in order to gather and synthesize information about our topic. These seven subactivities also provided opportunities to strengthen reading skills, build vocabulary, practice summarizing and questioning skills, and assess the students.

We used an excellent book, . . . *If You Traveled on the Underground Railroad* (Levine, 1988), one volume in Scholastic's series of nonfiction books that teach how children lived long ago. It is written at a third-grade reading level in a question-and-answer format. This book and the others in the series were particularly appealing to my students because they are written from a child's point of view.

The second book we used is called *Barefoot: Escape on the Underground Railroad* (Edwards, 1997). This moving and beautifully illustrated picture book provides children with a vivid sense of the many dangers and hardships faced by runaway slaves, as well as their tremendous courage and determination.

These two standards apply to the following seven activities.

Goal 2, Standard 2   To use English to achieve academically in all content areas: Students will use English to obtain, process, construct, and provide subject matter information in spoken and written form.

Descriptors

- listening to, speaking, reading, and writing about subject matter information
- gathering information orally and in writing
- retelling information
- responding to the work of peers and others
- formulating and asking questions

Progress Indicators

- write a summary of a chapter of a book
- locate information appropriate to an assignment in text
- edit and revise own written assignments
- use contextual clues
- generate and ask questions
- synthesize, analyze, and evaluate information
- explain change in characters in literature

Goal 2, Standard 3   To use English to achieve academically in all content areas: Students will use appropriate learning strategies to construct and apply academic knowledge.

Descriptors

- applying basic reading comprehension skills such as skimming, scanning, previewing, and reviewing text
- using context to construct meaning
- actively connecting new information to information previously learned
- planning how to and when to use cognitive strategies and applying them appropriately to a learning task

Progress Indicators

- verbalize relationships between new information and information previously learned in another setting
- scan an entry in a book to locate information for an assignment
- rephrase, explain, revise, and expand oral or written information to check comprehension

Group Read-Aloud and Discussion

This activity provided my students with sorely needed background information about our topic. It also facilitated practice in decoding and reading comprehension.

PROCEDURE

- Each student had a copy of . . . *If You Traveled on the Underground Railroad* (Levine, 1988). I read the one-page introduction to the book while they followed along. Afterwards, I posed simple questions to make sure that the students understood the text.

- After this reading, students volunteered to read aloud from the first chapter, "What Was the Underground Railroad?" and another chapter called "What Did It Mean to Be a Slave?" Because there was such enthusiasm about reading aloud, we adopted a round-robin approach, and everyone took a turn reading one paragraph.

- As we read together, I stopped periodically to clarify and ask questions to ensure comprehension.

Although I do not ask poor readers to read aloud, they usually insist on it: "Ms. DeFabbia, can we read? Please?" I remind them to use word-attack strategies as needed (e.g., picture, context, structural, and phonic clues) and to attend carefully to punctuation. Without this prompting, many students stumbled through the text, saying one word after another with no regard for periods, commas, or question marks, so meaning was totally lost. These read-alouds gave me ongoing insight into students' reading difficulties, strengths, and strategies, and allowed me to informally monitor progress.

Vocabulary Development

During the reading, I encouraged students to identify unfamiliar words and concepts and try to decipher their meaning using contextual and picture clues. This helped expand the students' vocabulary and strengthened their word-attack skills.

PROCEDURE

- As they read, I asked students to point out unfamiliar words. Through discussion and use of a dictionary when needed, we developed simple definitions. The students wrote these on paper that they kept in their work folders.

- The following day, and on many subsequent days, I started my lessons with a quick (5- to 10-minute) game to review the words learned in previous classes. Besides providing needed review and reinforcement for the students, this was also an assessment activity, letting me know when reteaching was necessary. Here is one game that really made my students giggle: I taped a word to a student's forehead without allowing him or her to see it. The rest of the group provided clues about the word until the one with the sticky forehead figured it out, as the following dialogue illustrates: "Someone who run away," offered Ngan. "They break the law," Amanda added. "Oh, I know: *fugitive!*" yelled Ricardo proudly. Lots of silliness and a great deal of vocabulary learning resulted from this activity.

- We played many other word games, and I constantly tried to provide variety so as to keep the interest level high. Variations included the following:

    1. One student picked a word out of a hat and gave clues while the others figured out the word.

    2. I gave clues, and the group of students figured out the word.

    3. We played in teams, with one team giving the clues and the other team figuring out the word.

    4. I provided words and definitions, and the students worked with partners to match them.

    5. I read sentences aloud, and the students filled in the blank words.

Summarizing and Questioning

The **reciprocal teaching** techniques described below helped strengthen reading comprehension. The techniques encouraged students to interact with and look more deeply into the text as they tried to ask difficult questions in order to outwit their classmates. The students also had a lot of good practice in formulating questions.

PROCEDURE

- After reading a chapter of the book together, I asked the students to use their own words to retell what they had read.

- The students asked each other questions based on the reading. These questions ranged from those for which the specific answer was actually in the passage to questions for which the students had to infer the answer. The students worked independently to generate and ask questions, but this can also be done in pairs or teams.

When I first used these techniques in this unit and other units, I had not yet learned about reciprocal teaching. I realized later that I was already applying many of the same techniques. (See Houghton Mifflin's Grade 3 Extra Support Handbook, 1997, for additional guidance on reciprocal teaching.)

Assessment

I wanted to see if the students could express their new knowledge in writing as well as orally, and I thought this assignment would help reinforce the historical information that we had been studying.

PROCEDURE

- I prepared a sheet of four questions relating to our reading, which the students answered in writing. When we had class discussions about the readings and related

From time to time, classroom teachers approach me with concerns about a student's progress or skills. For example, one teacher was troubled that a student did not write responses to test questions in complete, comprehensible sentences. Because I wanted my students to be well prepared for test taking, I planned a minilesson on this topic and structured the assessment questions to be answered accordingly. One student who had been particularly weak in structuring sentences showed some growth in grasping this concept. His answers indicated that he understood the questions, and they were more coherent than those he had written for the classroom teacher.

issues, it was hard to assess individual students' understanding; this activity provided me with a tool to assess individual learners' knowledge of key concepts. It also helped me see how well the students could express their newfound knowledge in writing.

- The students completed the assessment independently in class, and then we reviewed them as a group. The students demonstrated very good understanding of the information covered. Duong's question worksheet is shown below.

Question Worksheet

Name

The Underground Railroad

Answer the questions using complete sentences. Use the words from the questions to form your answers.

Example: Was the Underground Railroad a real railroad?

Answer: No, the Underground Railroad was not a real railroad.

1. What was the Underground Railroad?
The Underground Railroad was for the people to eacape from the master.

2. What were the houses called that the slaves hid in along the way?
The houses was called stations were slaves hid.

3. What was the job of a conductor?
The Job for conductor was to lead the slaves to the next station.

4. Why did people travel on the Underground Railroad?
They travel on the Underground railroad because noone cant see them. and because they want and they want eacape freedom good.

Independent Reading and Writing

After so much group reading and oral work, I wanted to give the students practice in reading and writing on their own. This activity allowed the students to explore their personal interests as they learned more about the Underground Railroad. It also strengthened communication skills as they presented their findings to their peers.

PROCEDURE

- I read aloud all the chapter titles from *. . . If You Traveled on the Underground Railroad*. The students chose one topic they were most interested in and read this chapter independently. Chapters they chose to write about included "Who Worked on the Underground Railroad?", "How Did Owners Try to Catch the Fugitives?", "Would You Use Disguises When You Ran Away?", "What Dangers Did You Face?", "Were There Special Hiding Places on the Underground Railroad?", and "How Would You Trick the Slave Hunters?" Taken together, these topics created a rich pool of information to flesh out the group's knowledge of the Underground Railroad.

- After reading, the students spent another 2 days writing, editing with my help, and revising a summary of their topics.

- Finally, the students read their summaries aloud to the whole group in our sharing circle. Besides sharing their writing, the students were effectively teaching each other about their topics. The students commented on the pieces and offered compliments to the writers, such as "I like the way you read"; "Your writing is interesting"; and "You did a good job explaining that."

I often end writing assignments with this type of sharing. Before we begin, we review how to be good listeners. We also verbally list the types of positive comments they could make after others read, such as those mentioned at left. I insist on undivided attention from each student. I find this activity offers a needed opportunity for the students to present their work aloud and to receive positive reinforcement in a safe setting.

ASSESSMENT

One of the strengths I saw in Duong's summary (shown on p. 95) was his comprehensive description of the many types of people who worked on the Underground Railroad. I also thought it was good that, even though he had started out copying straight from the book, he shifted to using his own words to summarize what he read. One area I decided to focus on was Duong's use of commas. He showed that he had some idea of how to do this, but he was not consistent. Also, like many students his age, he tended to write sentences that were strings of many different ideas connected by the word *and*. We had to work on developing clear, concise sentences that included correct capitalization and punctuation.

In Ngan's summary (shown on p. 95), the sentences were much clearer than Duong's, but the summary was less informative. She chose to include only two ways that slave owners tried to catch runaways. I saw Ngan as being a much more cautious writer than Duong and as being less willing to elaborate, which requires taking risks. I worked on encouraging her to include more details in her subsequent writing projects. Also, like many of my Vietnamese students, Ngan's writing showed that she struggled with plurals and verb tenses. This was also true in her speaking and in her reading aloud. Throughout the year, I taught minilessons to address these common errors.

Duong's Chapter Summary

Who worked on the Underground Railroad

   All kinds of people. Blacks and whites, children and adults, women and men and Harriet Tobman teachers and station master Storekeepers, housewives, carpenters and famous people help toBut some Conductors and the other blacks came to help the people runaway slave to have freedom. and some friends helped too.

Picture Book Read-Aloud

I wanted to provide another source of information about the Underground Railroad to strengthen and expand my students' understanding. I also thought it important to present the topic through another genre, a fictional picture book.

PROCEDURE

- I introduced the book *Barefoot: Escape on the Underground Railroad* (Edwards, 1997) by asking the students to look at the cover and predict what the story would be about from the title, the illustration, and what they

---

Ngan's Chapter Summary

How did owners try to catch the fugitives

   Most owners put advertisement in the newspaper. Some owners tells the paddyrollers take dogs to find it

---

had already learned. "A slave running away!" volunteered Ngan. "He's going to a station," chimed in Ricardo. "It's the nighttime," added Elizabeth. My students were pleased with themselves because they now had some knowledge of the subject, and they were anxious and excited to hear me read this new book to them.

- Because I had just one copy of the book, I read it aloud very slowly, asking many questions along the way. These questions required the students to interpret and analyze the information in the story. For example, the character in the book is referred to as "the Barefoot." The students had to determine who "the Barefoot" was and explain why he was referred to in this manner.

Shortly after we read this book, Duong's classroom teacher used it, too. She reported to me that his hand constantly shot up with answers to her questions. Usually a poor student, he was extremely pleased and proud to finally be able to feel so confident in class.

- After this slow reading, I read the book again. This time, I read the book straight through without stopping so that the students could hear and appreciate the story as a whole piece of literature.

- The students then wanted to study the illustrations in the book. The details they found here helped support many of the facts they were learning about the runaway slaves' experiences. For example, Ricardo said, "Look, there's the berries he ate," and Ngan commented, "They use the quilt to tell him it safe. We read it in the other book, too!"

I try to create many opportunities to read picture books to older students. They really appreciate a well-told story, and they love lingering over the illustrations to find all the subtle details that younger children might miss. This was especially true with this book, with its darkened, nighttime pictures.

What We Learned

This activity served as a summarizing tool. I wanted the students to think consciously about what they had learned and to put it down on paper in an organized manner so that they could use the summary as a guide during the game-making portion of the unit. Although we did not actually return to the K-W-L chart from the start of the unit to fill in the *L* column, it served a similar purpose.

Procedure

- I asked the students to think back and list all the things they had learned so far about the Underground Railroad. I modeled this activity with the whole group by starting the list with them.

- The students worked in pairs to add new items to the list. Generating this list was a difficult task for my students. "I can't think of nothing," moaned Elizabeth. "I don't know what to write," Ricardo complained. Although I had already seen through our other activities that the students had clearly absorbed a great deal of information, it was a challenge for them to isolate this knowledge and articulate it in the way I was asking.

- Afterwards, we came back together as a group and compiled a long list of information on chart paper. Much of our list was actually generated at this point, with me providing lots of help by asking very leading questions. When we were finally done, and especially after I had typed the list and

I think it is worthwhile for teachers to provide more practice with this type of activity. Students are often asked to answer questions or fill in blanks to demonstrate knowledge. Learning to summarize what they have learned can be a positive experience as it develops higher order thinking and gives students practice in assessing their own learning, a very important skill that is often neglected in schools.

What We Learned

Things we know about the Underground Railroad

The Underground Railroad was a secret way for slaves to escape.

Sometimes it took a long time for people to travel on it.

People used it to get to the North.

Sometimes people got caught.

People were breaking the law.

Sometimes families were split up.

Frederick Douglass and Harriet Tubman were involved with the Underground Railroad.

People traveled at night.

People ate wild berries.

Safe houses were called "stations."

Quilts and other signals were used to help slaves find the safe houses.

Animals helped the runaway slaves.

People who helped slaves were called "conductors".

All kinds of people worked on the railroad: black and white, housewives, storekeepers, carpenters and famous people.

Slaves used special hiding places such as trap doors and hidden tunnels, sliding panels covered by pictures, secret compartments and false bottoms in wagons.

Owners tried to catch slaves by putting ads in newspapers and hiring slave catchers.

Slaves faced many dangers, like being caught, being recognized by people who knew them, being attacked by wild animals in the forest such as alligators and bears.

Slaves used disguises such as dressing up like a boy if you were a girl or dressing up like a girl if you were a boy, and pretended to be different people than they were. Some pretended they were in a funeral procession.

given copies to the students, they were amazed to see how much they had actually learned about the Underground Railroad. "What We Learned" shows the list of what the class had learned (see p. 97).

Final Group-Project Activities

Learning About Games

At this point in our unit, I shifted the focus away from the Underground Railroad to games. Because the students would make a game for the unit's final project, I wanted to spend some time thinking analytically about games. This week-long activity was enjoyable for the students, but it also involved using many critical thinking skills, the development of which is a goal highly emphasized in our school.

> ***Goal 2, Standard 1***   **To use English to achieve academically in all content areas: Students will use English to interact in the classroom.**
>
> ### *Descriptors*
> * following oral and written directions, implicit and explicit
> * participating in full-class, group, and pair discussions
> * expressing likes, dislikes, and needs
> * negotiating and managing interaction to accomplish a task
>
> ### *Progress Indicators*
> * follow directions to learn and play games
> * ask the teacher to restate or simplify directions
> * share classroom materials and work successfully in a group
> * negotiate cooperative roles and task assignments
> * take turns when speaking in a group
> * participate in class discussions

PROCEDURE

* I asked the students to name all the board games they could think of. What enthusiasm! After we had made a long list on the board, I asked the question, "What makes a good game?" Now they had to think. "What do you mean? It's just fun," said Kham. "But what makes it fun?" I pressed. We listed their answers on the board: "interesting," "lots of action," "exciting," "lots of things in it," "colorful," and, of course, "winning."

* Next, we played games. I started with the simple, familiar game *Candyland* (1984). We read the directions, learned them, and then played together. This activity helped build a sense of community among the group.

* I gave the students a set of questions for analyzing and evaluating the game. These required an explanation and definition of terms before they could be understood. We reviewed and answered the questions together. Amanda's worksheet (on p. 99) shows the questions that the students had to answer.

Amanda's Worksheet

Learning About Board Games

1. Game name: Hangman

2. What is the <u>concept</u>, or <u>theme</u>, of the game?
(what is it about?) It is about that you gess a letter
and say a word.

3. How is the game designed? What does it look like?
The game Looks Like fun. It has coors, Letters and a board.
It has a dial.

4. What is the <u>object</u> of the game? Describe how
you play the game. This is how to play the Game you have
Letters in a box and a board than You pick a word and Stick
it on the top and the other person gesses what word you have.
And how I now I won is Just following along and playing and
shareing.

5. Is the game fun, interesting, or challenging?
What makes it so? It in intresting because
it has fun parts and colors it is intresting because it is a game.
gessing ,ofun.

6. Does this game need luck or skill? Explain.
I think it is Luck because when something Rolls You have
good Luck. and we use are brain

- We repeated this process with a wonderful cooperative game called *The Secret Door* (1991) and with the board game version of the familiar *Hangman* (1988). In playing *The Secret Door,* the students worked with partners to answer the questions, but in playing *Hangman,* they worked alone. Both times, the whole group came back together

As we repeatedly used the new terms on the question sheet, the students became very familiar and comfortable with them. By the end of this activity, they had incorporated these words and concepts into their working vocabularies. This became evident as we worked on our final game-making project, described below.

afterwards to discuss their answers. Lively discussions often ensued ("It's skill because we all win together," argued Ngan about *The Secret Door.* "No, you need luck," insisted Duong). I was impressed with the level of understanding some students displayed, as when Ngan wrote about *Hangman*, "Skill and luck because first we guess that is luck and the rest are skill."

Making Our Game

Now that the students were knowledgeable about the Underground Railroad, and had played and analyzed several different games, it was time to begin making our own game. This provided an opportunity for the students to concretely apply, and for me to assess, what they had learned about the topic and about games. I wanted them to have fun. I hoped, too, that the game would reveal their newly acquired knowledge about the Underground Railroad and also about what makes games enjoyable and interesting. It was a wonderful and challenging opportunity for students to work together as a team. The project, which took almost 2 weeks to complete, required much discussion, negotiation, and cooperation on the part of all students.

> *Goal 2, Standard 1* To use English to achieve academically in all content areas: Students will use English to interact in the classroom.

> ### Descriptors
>
> - participating in full-class, group, and pair discussions
> - negotiating and managing interaction to accomplish tasks
> - explaining actions
> - elaborating and extending other people's ideas and words
> - expressing likes, dislikes, and needs
>
> ### Progress Indicators
>
> - use polite forms to negotiate and reach consensus
> - negotiate cooperative roles and task assignments
> - take turns when speaking in a group
> - modify a statement made by a peer
> - listen to and incorporate peer and teacher feedback in performing tasks
> - share classroom materials and work successfully with a partner and in a large group

PROCEDURE

- Brainstorming was the first task in this game-making process. The students had to decide, as a group, what they wanted the game to be like and look like. Their lively discussion, with some guidance, produced the following ideas: "Slaves run away from the slavery" (Ngan); "They traveling in the Underground Railroad" (Elizabeth); "It should go on a road to the North"

(Kham); "You find the North Star, then you win!" (Ricardo); and "Things happen when they running away" (Ngan).

- I asked the students to visualize how they thought the game should look. Ricardo drew a very rough sketch on the board, and the students nodded in agreement.

- After reviewing our previously created list of things learned about the Underground Railroad (see p. 97), the students worked in pairs to develop ideas on how to include this information in the game. I suggested they start by making a list of good and bad things that could happen to a slave trying to escape. Amanda's list (below) and Ngan's list (on p. 102) each show examples of the points generated by two pairs of students. Both listed positive and negative things that could happen to

I was very impressed with how well the students shared thoughts, listened to each other, and built upon each other's ideas. At the start of this process, neither the students nor I had a clear notion of what the game should be like. Nevertheless, they were able to reach consensus on the basic concept and design of the game fairly quickly.

I find that few of my students know how to write lists. Instead, they painstakingly write long, complete sentences for each item. I now know to start such activities with a 3-minute minilesson on how to write ideas in short, bulleted phrases.

Amanda's List

March 20, 1998

ESOL Room   Mrs DaFabbia

Good

1. animals helped the slaves to escape.

2. The people would win by getting to the stations"

3.

4.

bad

1. people could get caught you go back and start.

2. people were breaking the law.

3 Sometimes people get caught by slave catchers owners move back to start.

4. bad People were looking for slaves.

Ngan's List

> railroad
> on the Underground ⌃
>
> good
> 1. place to rest ; - question. What place you would rest?
>
> 2. find the big dipper ; - go up three spaces.
>
> bad
> 3. wild animals ; - go back three spaces.
>
> 4. step on nail ; - stay there to something happen.
> on nail
> Example: like you step, but that say roll the dies
> three time and that three time you have to
> get all 5 number, then you got to move.
>
> 1. In the game, A long the road, like we write
> the place one three spot then ask the question

slaves, as well as suggestions for how these events could be represented on the board. For example, Amanda wrote on her "bad" list, "sometimes people get caught by slave catchers [and] owners, move back to start."

- We agreed on the tasks still needing to be accomplished, and the students divided into two groups. One group worked on transforming the lists of good and bad things into appropriate game language. The other drew a draft of the game onto paper and then transferred it to the poster board that I provided.

- At the end of each class period, the groups shared their accomplishments with each other. The students commented on and provided

When grouping students, I try to pair those with varying abilities. The more linguistically advanced students help the others with spelling, grammar, and the appropriate language to use in a particular context, and more intellectually talented students can help others grasp the concepts. For example, Ngan, a very bright student who was usually the first to understand the requirements of a task and do what was asked of her, was more limited in her ability to express herself using the conventions of English than most of the others in this group. I often paired her with Elizabeth, whose abilities and limitations were the opposite.

feedback to their peers, who either made changes accordingly or occasionally argued why it should be their way.

- I asked the students to think about writing the rules and directions for the game. Although they had definite ideas about how the game should be played, they found it much more difficult to translate their thoughts into appropriate language.

This part of the unit did not always go very smoothly. The class period was short, and, often, by the time the students figured out what they needed to do, got supplies, and became truly involved in a task, it was time to go. I was also unsure whether to provide more direction or let the students figure out for themselves how to tackle this challenging new activity. In retrospect, I could have provided a bit more structure, assigning more specific tasks and telling the students what to do next. Yet I also saw value in letting the students struggle through the process independently.

- I helped a great deal with formulating the wording. My students tended to use long, involved sentences to explain how to play a game, so we looked back at how instructions for other games were worded. I asked the students to think of sentences explaining how to play the game. Then we practiced changing them into "instructions language." For example, the original sentence, "First you have to roll the die and see what number you have and then go along the game and stop and do what it says" became "To Play: 1) Roll the die; 2) Move the number of spaces it says on the die. 3) When you land on a square with writing, follow the instructions."

- Finally, we had a finished product and were ready to play the game. I explained that this was an editing activity. We would see how the game worked, and think about any needed changes or improvements.

Actually finishing and playing the game was tremendously exciting for my students, who had worked so long and hard on this project. I believe that because this process challenged them so much, they felt particularly proud of their accomplishment.

- After playing, the students decided to change the rules a bit and to add a few more obstacles along the game's path to make it more challenging. A copy of the game board is shown on page 104.

Sharing Feelings and Sharing the Game

My initial idea for a culminating activity was to ask the students to write process essays telling all the steps involved in making the game. I hoped for a solid writing piece to complement all the oral language development and artwork. However, my students made it clear that they were done with this lengthy project, so I decided to simplify the writing assignment significantly.

I also felt it was extremely important for my students to share this game with their families and mainstream classmates. Public recognition is crucial for students' self-esteem, and I believe it is important for our work in the classroom to have a greater purpose and a broader audience than just having it assessed by the teacher. Because the students knew in advance that they would be sharing this game outside our ESL class,

Game Board

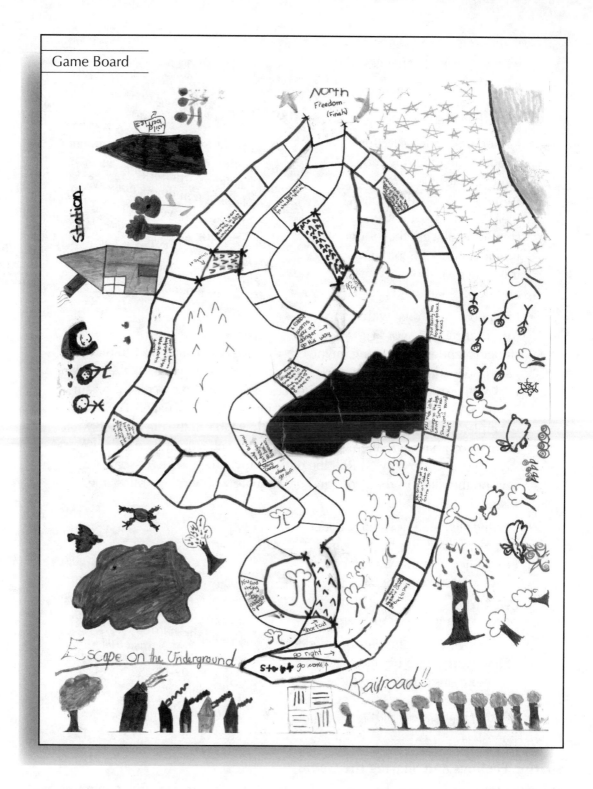

they seemed to work harder and more conscientiously to make it something about which they could feel proud.

PROCEDURE

- The students wrote short essays expressing their feelings about the project. I asked them to be honest and not to worry about offending me with something negative. The essays were not edited but were left as they were in order to keep the activity brief.

Goal 1, Standard 1 To use English to communicate in social settings: Students will use English to participate in social interactions.

Descriptors

- sharing and requesting information
- expressing needs, feelings, and ideas
- engaging in conversations

Sample Progress Indicators

- write personal essays
- engage listeners' attention verbally or nonverbally
- clarify and restate information as needed
- teach classmates how to play a game
- describe feelings and emotions after doing a class project
- ask for permission from a teacher

- Most students chose to read their essays aloud to each other. To my surprise and great pleasure, one aspect of this project that several students enjoyed was working as a team. This had been one of my goals, and it simply had not occurred to me that it was important to the students as well. Ngan's essay and Duong's essay are shown on page 106.

This sharing seemed to make all the hard work worthwhile to my students. After everyone had taken turns bringing the game to their classrooms and homes, most asked to have second turns. They played the game frequently, which was very satisfying for me.

- The students took turns sharing the game in their mainstream classrooms. First, they described the project to their teachers and asked permission to teach it to and play it with their classmates. It became a popular free-time classroom activity. Several of the teachers complimented me on the students' excellent work.

- The students later took the game home to play with their families.

Additional Information

The completion of the game involved making many decisions, drawing, writing, decorating, and engaging in lots of conversation: "It should be three spaces go back, not two." "What color do we make the safe houses?" "How can it look like nighttime?" "I know, put stars and moons!" "Yuck, that swamp be ugly!" "How do you spell *conductor*?"

While the students were busy working on various pieces of the game, I facilitated the process by making sure all the students were busy, that they were listening to each

---

Ngan's Essay

ESOL

4/6/98
Ms. DeFabb...

This game is about Escape on the underground Railroad. We cooperation and work together. It is fun working on a game but it a little bit hard. I feel great about this game beause we did team work.

---

other, and that they were paying attention to important details. I kept a daily checklist to assess each student's involvement in this process, including the tangible work they produced each day and their level of involvement in conversations and providing feedback to each other. When one or two students were not showing enough involvement, I focused my attention on them by assigning specific tasks and soliciting their thoughts and opinions through direct questioning.

While listening to these conversations, I noticed that my students had really become a cohesive group. This realization (as well as seeing the game develop) was extremely gratifying for me. I also could observe their learning in the various obstacles and positive encounters they incorporated into the game, in the way they structured the paths to run northward, in the details of their drawings, and in the types of comments they made to each other. Their game revealed a tremendous amount of knowledge about the Underground Railroad. I could tell by how hard they worked to make this game enjoyable, challenging, and attractive that the time spent playing and analyzing other games had been worthwhile. This was the best type of assessment I could imagine: The students had to apply knowledge and actively demonstrate learning.

Duong's Essay

I feel great because we work together and we worked like a big group and mrs. Defabbia was proud of us. because we worked together and we aid lots of thing to it and we had fun playing it and Mrs Defabbia let one people take to the class room for thier class to play and descabe it like it a nice game and the game was called Escape on the underground Railroad.

When I think about assessing the specific growth of my students, one boy in particular comes to mind. For me, Ricardo was definitely the most difficult student in this group. He often complained about having to come to my class each day. While there, he was moody, disruptive, and immature. Ricardo always found a way to get attention, usually negative. His mother's interventions would help for a few days, but then he would revert to his previous behavior.

This unit motivated Ricardo in a way that changed him and our relationship for the rest of the school year. Playing games in class was what first piqued his interest. Although this did not surprise me much, I was quite amazed with the way his enthusiasm continued throughout the rest of the unit and the school year. Without realizing it, I had created the opportunity for Ricardo to channel his energy into providing real leadership during the game-making process. He was the first to conceive the game's format, and he especially enjoyed doing the artwork. His involvement went much further; he often spoke up and provided useful feedback and opinions to his peers. I could see his confidence grow as the weeks went on, and I also observed that the other students began to regard him as a leader rather than a distraction. He came to class excited and ready to work each day, and his behavior problems became history. This was a critical turnaround for Ricardo and a revealing experience for me. Although I had already known this intellectually, it became crystal clear to me how important it is to find effective ways to motivate and engage students, especially the more challenging ones.

Conclusion

The following year, Duong was the only student from this group remaining with me in ESL. Amanda and Ngan tested out, and the other three students moved to different city schools. From time to time throughout the school year, Duong would ask, "Ms. DeFabbia, can we make a game again?" He would tell the other ESOL students about our project, and I could hear in his voice that it was one of the best school experiences he had ever had.

Looking back, I realize it was also one of the best experiences I have had in my teaching career. I learned so much about motivating students and group dynamics. I discovered that I could effectively take control of a difficult classroom situation and turn it completely around. I experienced authentic assessment at its best. I developed more confidence in my teaching, and I strengthened my belief that students really want to be challenged and held to high standards.

RESOURCES

Children's Literature

Edwards, P. D. (1997). *Barefoot: Escape on the Underground Railroad.* New York: HarperCollins.

Levine, E. (1988). *. . . . If you traveled on the Underground Railroad.* New York: Scholastic.

Games

Candyland. (1984). Springfield, MA: Milton Bradley.
    A very simple board game that requires no reading, Candyland *is a good example of a game that is based on pure luck.*

Hangman. (1988). Springfield, MA: Milton Bradley.
    This is the board version of a classic game.

The secret door. (1991). Perth, Canada: Family Pastimes.
    A great cooperative mystery game for ages 5 and up, this game is a cross between Clue *and* Memory.

Works Cited

Extra support handbook (Grade 3). (1997). Boston: Houghton Mifflin.

TESOL. (1997). *ESL standards for pre-K–12 students.* Alexandria, VA: Author.

The University of the State of New York, State Education Department. (1996). *Learning standards for English language arts.* Albany, NY: Author.

UNIT 5
The Most Beautiful Place in the World

LINDA NEW LEVINE

Introduction

There are seven third-grade children sitting around the semicircular table facing me. I am enthusiastically leading the children in a good morning song. The children are half-heartedly mumbling along with me.

Good Morning.
Hello.
Good Morning.
Hello.
How are you?
I'm OK.
How are you?
I feel fine.
Good Morning.
Hello.
Good Morning.
Hello.
How are you?
I feel great today.

This was another typical beginning to my class of third-grade ESOL students. I met with them every morning from 9:15 to 10:10, and each day began with an argument, tears, or

> **Context**
>
> Grade level: Third grade
> English proficiency level: Intermediate
> Native language of students: Spanish
> Focus of instruction: Language arts/social studies
> Type of class: Pullout ESL, 1 hour daily
> Length of unit: 1 month

inertia, which made it a very difficult class to teach. I began the singing in an effort to start our school day in an upbeat way.

This was a class of children who had many problems. Rudy, Bryan, and Roberto met regularly with the school psychologist because of emotional difficulties, such as hyperactivity or aggressiveness. Several of the children also had physical problems, such as asthma, which had kept them out of school quite a bit. None of the children was doing well in learning to read and write in English. The children were grouped together because of their fluency in oral English and their lack of success in reading and writing. The previous year's norm-referenced standardized test scores indicated that the children's normal curve equivalent (NCE) scores ranged from 1 to 43.

The children were all from Spanish-speaking families. Bryan, Jorge, Francisco, Maureen, and Cindy were born in the district to parents from Guatemala, Ecuador, Chile, Panama, and Spain. Roberto was born in Spain and had enrolled in our school in the second grade; he had some experience reading in Spanish. Rudy was born in Panama to a Panamanian mother and a bilingual American father. He had enrolled in our school in September after having spent time in California and Florida in a variety of schools. Rudy could not read in any language.

The good morning song always put me into a more positive mood, and I was beginning to see signs that the children were getting into it, too. I was always searching for ways to help the children develop their academic and social skills. This search led to the unit that I describe here.

Unit Overview

I taught this language arts/social studies unit, named after a book we read together, toward the end of the school year. It took about a month to complete. We had spent the year working on basic decoding and comprehension skills and reading shorter pieces of fiction and nonfiction, and I thought the students were ready to read a longer piece of fiction. *The Most Beautiful Place in the World* (Cameron, 1988) is a short novel that takes place in Guatemala. It tells of Juan, a young boy who longs to attend school and learn to read. The novel is one of three chapter books that third-grade students are required to read in my school district. I felt that the spring was a good time to introduce *The Most Beautiful Place in the World,* as it tied together some of the content studied in the students' third-grade classrooms and integrated information about their native countries and language.

The novel incorporates many Spanish words and foods, and many aspects of Hispanic culture. My students rarely used Spanish during the school day, although I knew it was used in their homes. The children had disowned their culture within the school community, refusing to admit to their teachers that they spoke Spanish. The exception was Roberto, who had emigrated from Spain in the second grade. Roberto had a solid vocabulary in Spanish, could read and write in Spanish, and often helped his classroom teacher with Spanish translations of English words. He was proud of his country and his bilingualism. I hoped the classroom reading experience would encourage more of my students to feel proud of who they were and what they knew.

The third-grade classroom teachers were leading the students through a research project during this same time. Each child had chosen an animal to research and describe in a long piece of writing. Many of my students had chosen jungle animals from their native countries. The jungle is one of the four geographical regions studied in our third-grade social studies curriculum. I knew I could integrate information about jungle regions into our discussions about Guatemala.

Unit Overview: The Most Beautiful Place in the World

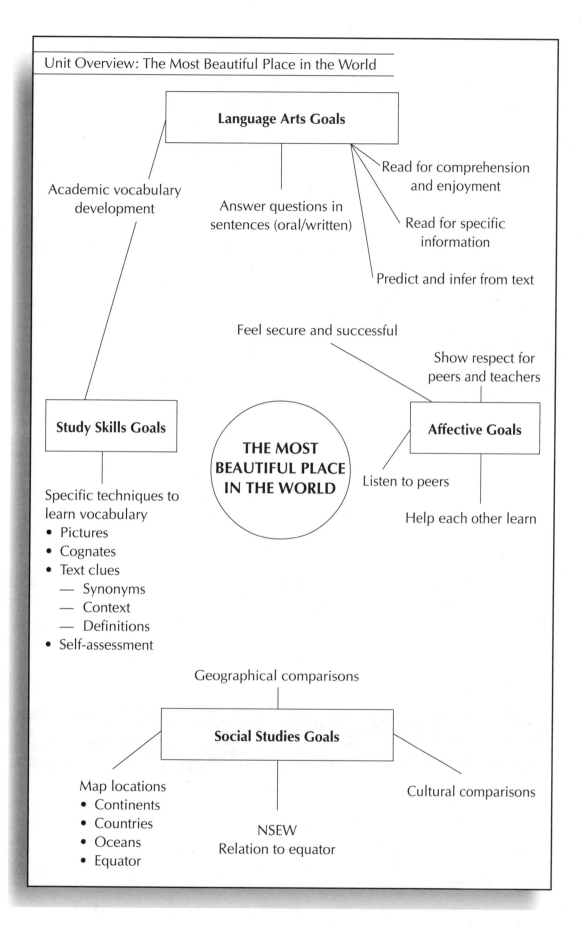

Language Arts Goals

Academic vocabulary development

Answer questions in sentences (oral/written)

Read for comprehension and enjoyment

Read for specific information

Predict and infer from text

Feel secure and successful

Show respect for peers and teachers

Study Skills Goals

THE MOST BEAUTIFUL PLACE IN THE WORLD

Affective Goals

Listen to peers

Help each other learn

Specific techniques to learn vocabulary
- Pictures
- Cognates
- Text clues
  — Synonyms
  — Context
  — Definitions
- Self-assessment

Geographical comparisons

Social Studies Goals

Map locations
- Continents
- Countries
- Oceans
- Equator

NSEW
Relation to equator

Cultural comparisons

I hoped that the students would feel a sense of accomplishment and pride by completing a chapter book that their friends in the mainstream classroom were also reading. I hoped that they would begin to feel more pride in their native cultures and language. I also hoped that these positive feelings would affect the rather negative ways that some of the students behaved in school and with each other.

My goals for the unit addressed language arts, study skills, social studies, and affective factors. I graphed my goals before I started the unit and they looked something like the unit overview shown.

Standards

I did not think too much about standards when I first began to plan this unit. I thought more about the cognitive, content, and affective needs of the students. Once I had begun, however, I went back to *ESL Standards for Pre-K–12 Students* (TESOL, 1997), which is always on my desk. I was fairly familiar with Goal 2 (To use English to achieve academically). This had been my main focus for this particular class all year because of the students' struggles with reading and writing. However, I wanted to include some affective goals that I felt were critically important for children who may be emotionally and learning disabled. I discovered that Goal 3 (To use English in socially and culturally appropriate ways) was closely related to my own goals of showing respect and assisting others in learning.

I had no idea how to assess these affective goals, however, as they seemed a little vague to me initially. When I browsed through the companion volume, *Scenarios for ESL Standards-Based Assessment* (TESOL, in press), I noticed examples of checklists and remembered that I had used these with beginning-level language learners to good effect. I devised a checklist that helped me monitor progress in the affective goals for my unit.

Activities

K-W: What Do We Know About Guatemala?

I began the unit by activating what the children already knew about Guatemala and sharing what they knew (*K*) and wanted to know (*W*) on a K-W-L chart. I felt this would hook them into wanting to read the book because some of the students were already quite knowledgeable. Bryan, for example, had visited his grandparents in Guatemala the summer before.

> *Goal 2, Standard 1* **To use English to achieve academically in all content areas: Students will use English to interact in the classroom.**
>
> ### Descriptors
> - participating in group discussion
> - elaborating and extending other people's ideas and words
>
> ### Progress Indicators
> - join in a group discussion at the appropriate time and in an appropriate manner
> - listen to and respond to a peer's comments

Goal 2, Standard 2 To use English to achieve academically in all content areas: Students will use English to obtain, process, construct, and provide subject matter information in spoken and written form.

Descriptor

- formulating and asking questions

Progress Indicator

- generate and ask questions about unknown information

PROCEDURE

- I asked the students to talk to their parents about the fact that we were going to read a book about Guatemala. If parents had any pictures, objects, or mementos of Guatemala, I hoped they would let their children bring them in to share with the class.

- The next day, Bryan was the only student who had any information to share; he brought pictures, which he spoke about proudly for about 5 minutes.

- I passed out copies of *The Most Beautiful Place in the World* (Cameron, 1988) and asked the students to examine the picture on the front cover. We also riffled through the pictures in the book and read the paragraph on the back cover for further clues to Guatemala and the story itself. The students then told what they had learned about Guatemala.

- The next day, I distributed student notebooks and modeled how to divide the page into two halves. On a large chart on the front easel, I labeled each half of the page to resemble a K-W chart:

What I Know	What I Want to Know
About Guatemala	About Guatemala

- I asked the students to tell what they knew and remembered from our discussion about Guatemala. I wrote the information on the class chart in the *What I Know About Guatemala* column and the students copied it into their notebooks. We then discussed what they wanted to know about Guatemala. I set a goal of at least one appropriate question from each student. I then wrote these questions in the second column, *What I Want to Know.* I planned to use the notebook charts later in the unit when I taught the students to write cohesive descriptive paragraphs about Guatemala. Maureen's K-W

Because I was concerned about the students' social skills, particularly whether they listened to each other in this kind of group discussion, I kept a social skills checklist. For example, while the students listened to Bryan, I noted who listened respectfully and listed brief examples of inappropriate behavior, such as calling out, using impolite language, or interrupting. Over time, these checklists helped me determine the students' progress and were essential in conferences with parents and classroom teachers.

Maureen's K-W Chart

What I know (Guatemala)	What I want to Know
There are five volcanoes.	Guatemala is located in Central America?
There are Indian temples.	
people speak spanish.	Which ocean is nearby?
The climate is hot.	Which is the capitol city?
The money is called "Quezales".	Where does th President live?
Quezales is a bird with blue plumage.	What kind of clothes do they wear?
Children wear uniforms to school.	

chart, which is shown, helped me see that she was still having difficulty copying from a chart, but she was more successful at copying written text than she had been at the beginning of the year, when she had rarely included punctuation or capitalization.

The Geography of Guatemala

The third-grade social studies curriculum in my district emphasizes several geographic concepts that the children had been exposed to in their classrooms but that I was not satisfied they completely understood. I knew from previous lessons with this group, for example, that although most of the students knew which countries their parents came from, their notion of *country* in relation to *continent* was fuzzy. Also, I was not sure they understood the relationship among North, Central, and South America. Some of the children seemed to need more practice working with a compass rose and directionality. The introduction of *The Most Beautiful Place in the World* gave me the opportunity to revisit these concepts. The social studies objectives came from my district's third-grade curriculum:

- World communities can be located on maps and globes.
- The spatial relationships of world communities can be described by location, direction, distance, and scale.
- Regions represent areas of the Earth's surface with unifying geographic characteristics.
- The Earth's continents and oceans can be located in relation to each other and to principal parallels and meridians. (Bedford Central School District, n.d., p. 2)

Goal 2, Standard 2 **To use English to achieve academically in all content areas: Students will use English to obtain, process, construct, and provide subject matter information in spoken and written form.**

Descriptor

- listening to and speaking about subject matter information

Progress Indicator

- ask questions and respond using academic vocabulary and grammar

PROCEDURE

- I began the activity by putting a large map of the world on the table in front of the students. I gave them about 5 minutes to explore the map and to share information freely among themselves. (My students loved maps and enjoyed locating their native countries.)

- I then asked the students if they could locate Guatemala on the map. This took a little searching because Guatemala is rather small on my class map. During this activity, I modeled the language of directionality: *north of, south of*, and so forth. I also modeled the location phrase *Guatemala is located* . . . . These were elements of language that I wanted my students to use within a mapping context.

- Next, I distributed small, blank maps that incorporated North America, Central America, and South America. I asked the students to color-code the three regions and the two oceans. I suggested that they refer to the large wall map to decide where one region began and another ended. The students labeled the three regions in about 10 minutes.

When working with larger classes, I have found that it helps to place students in groups of four and prepare sample questions for them to use while playing question-and-answer games like these in their table groups. I then rotate the teacher role every 2–3 minutes.

- We spent the rest of the period playing a question-and-answer game using the little maps. I asked, "Where is the United States located?" and the students had to answer in complete sentences, for example, "The United States is located in North America." After a few questions like this, the students played teacher and took turns asking questions of the group.

- The next day, I gave the students copies of the same blank maps, but with the individual countries outlined. The students worked to color-code and label each country using the individual maps in the back of the Daily Assignment Agenda books used by the students in our school to keep track of daily assignments. For the rest of the period, we played Thumbs Up, Thumbs Down, a game in which the students had to use their country maps to determine if statements I made using location phrases were correct (thumbs up) or incorrect (thumbs down). For example, if I said, "Guatemala is located north of the United States," I expected the students to give the thumbs-down gesture. After modeling specific phrases, I asked students to play teacher. All of the children participated enthusiastically in this game.

  Using hand signals is a quick way to assess the comprehension of large numbers of students. Even though the children may try to peek at each other's signals, it is usually easy to detect. Initially, Jorge peeked a lot at other students rather than consulting his maps. I therefore moved nearer to him and helped out by pointing to the countries I was referring to orally. I think this helped him focus because soon he was consulting his map and indicating the correct answer.

- Assessment: While the students were playing Thumbs Up, Thumbs Down, I used a checklist to assess my students' ability to ask and to answer questions of location. The students noticed what I was doing, and they appeared to be motivated to work hard to provide correct questions and answers because they thought I was keeping score for the game. I simply used a list that I had already run off for this purpose and made shorthand notes on the area I was assessing. From this assessment, I determined that Jorge, Roberto, Rudy, and Maureen could use more practice with asking and answering questions of location, as the assessment checklist on page 117 shows.

- The next day, we spent another 15 minutes on map work. I knew from the day before that most of the children needed more practice with sentences indicating location. To introduce them to new content that they could then use for practicing the grammatical structure of focus, I asked Jorge, who comes from Ecuador, to locate his country on the map. I then asked for the name of the line running through his country. Bryan recalled the word *equator*. We compared the two words (*Ecuador* and *equator*) on the blackboard, and the students saw that they were similar. Using the globe, they noticed that the equator ran all around the globe and was directly in the center. I asked the students to talk to their **elbow buddies** to guess what the purpose of the equator might be. After a minute or two, the students each shared their buddies' ideas. Francisco and Cindy knew that the equator divided the globe in half. The other children got the same idea by

Assessment Checklist

Grade: 3   **Date:** MAY 12

Students:	INCORRECT QUESTIONS	INCORRECT ANSWERS
1. Jorge	✓	✓✓ (N, S, E, W ?)
2. Maureen	✓	✓✓ (north of ___ / South of ___)
3. Rudy	✓	✓✓ (east of ___ / ___ is west of ___)
4. Cindy	✓	
5. Roberto	✓	✓✓ (is located)
6. Bryan		
7. Francisco		

" ___ is located N S E W of ___ "

listening to the two of them talk about it. We then went around the group so the students could tell if their native countries were north or south of the equator. I modeled first, "My country, the United States of America, is located north of the equator." Writing this key phrase on the blackboard made it possible for the students to use it as a model to construct their own sentences.

- Assessment: I used one of my favorite assessment tools with this lesson: **ticket to leave.** Using this technique, I usually ask students to respond orally to a question before they may leave the classroom. On this day, I decided to ask the children to respond in writing instead. The students wrote in their notebooks, and after I had checked their writing, they were free to leave the class. It was a very motivating summarizing activity for my students and gave them a clear picture of what I expected them to know or be able to do at the end of the lesson. For this lesson, I wrote the following:

  Answer these questions in complete sentences:

  1. Which country is located north of Guatemala?

  2. Is Guatemala located in Central America or South America?

  3. Is Guatemala located north or south of the equator?

Ticket to leave can be used with a large class group if there are sufficient responses to match the class size. Some teachers accomplish this quickly by giving students Post-its on which to write their answers and collecting them at the door as the children leave the class. Asking questions orally is another way to use this assessment tool. It takes less time, and children are able to learn from listening to each other's answers.

All of the students were able to accomplish this task with ease. They used the key sentence on the blackboard as a scaffold to support their grammar and spelling. Roberto, Rudy, and Jorge did not have perfect spelling the first time around and had to correct a few words before they were able to earn their ticket to leave.

Vocabulary Learning

Vocabulary learning was an important goal in this unit. We had worked since the beginning of the year on decoding skills; this work was necessary because most of the students were still having difficulty with short vowel words, digraphs, and syllabication. Rudy was frustrated at the primer level of English reading, and Bryan, Jorge, and Maureen were barely at the first-grade level in reading. Because of their oral fluency in English, comprehension was less of a problem for the children until we began to read grade-level material with specific, difficult vocabulary.

Goal 2, Standard 2 **To use English to achieve academically in all content areas: Students will use English to obtain, process, construct, and provide subject matter information in spoken and written form.**

Descriptor

- understanding and producing technical vocabulary

Progress Indicator

- match and define vocabulary

Goal 2, Standard 3 **To use English to achieve academically in all content areas: Students will use appropriate learning strategies to construct and apply academic knowledge.**

Descriptors

- applying self-monitoring and self-correcting strategies to build and expand a vocabulary knowledge base
- evaluating one's own success in learning vocabulary

Progress Indicators

- assess one's own vocabulary understanding using a chart
- use picture clues to remember new vocabulary
- use synonyms and definitions within the text to understand new vocabulary

The Most Beautiful Place in the World (Cameron, 1988) has a reading level of 3.7. I anticipated that it would be very difficult for the group to understand without some support and that vocabulary would prove the biggest challenge. I planned to modify the reading of the book through large-group reading techniques so that decoding problems would be minimized.

I knew that the size of children's vocabulary is directly correlated with their reading abilities. I had been working on vocabulary development techniques for a couple of years with different groups of children, but I still was not satisfied with my ability to help students acquire large numbers of new words. Therefore, in this unit I placed a lot of emphasis on teaching strategies to help students comprehend and learn new vocabulary on their own.

PROCEDURE

- The daily vocabulary study throughout this unit usually came from a workbook called *Vocabulary Connections* (Sharpe & Sperry, 1997). The first unit we worked on involved words associated with the rain forest. We began each week with a shared reading using a technique called buzz reading. The students and I read together as a group, using quiet (buzz) voices. This technique enabled me to listen to the students as they read and note any decoding problems. My voice also provided support and correct pronunciation for difficult or new vocabulary. I asked the students to notice the words in heavy black print while reading because these were the words that I wanted them to learn and on which they would be tested at the end of the chapter.

- After finishing the reading, we went back to the first target word, and I asked the students to find clues in the text that helped define the word. They looked for synonyms, definitions, and context clues; underlined the clues; and shared them with each other. I then taught the students how to use the glossary at the back of the book. The homework for that night was to match new words with definitions. Our goal as a class was to achieve 100% on every homework activity.

- Assessment: I used the same reading vocabulary to match and write definitions for a few days each week, and at the end of that time, the students took a test from the book. This was exciting for them because I did not often use tests, and they were motivated to achieve 100% on the test. Bryan, Maureen, and Francisco began using the glossary at the back of the book to learn the words; subsequently they started to score 100% on the tests. I asked them to share with the class how they had learned to be successful, and they indicated that the glossary had helped. This encouraged Rudy, Roberto, and Cindy to begin using the glossary, too. Jorge took a little longer to catch on, but by the end of the unit, he, too, was achieving 100% on the vocabulary tests.

- After the first 15 minutes of work each day on *Vocabulary Connections* (Sharpe & Sperry, 1997), I used similar techniques to help the students learn the vocabulary in the chapter book: searching for synonyms, context clues, and

I stumbled across a motivating vocabulary-learning technique one day. A few students who returned to class after being absent had missed the test that week. I asked Rudy and Bryan to buddy up with and teach the test to a child who had been absent. The boys worked hard at helping the other child achieve 100% on the test. I was amazed to see these often-difficult children work very well together one-on-one. They were helpful and nurturing. I reminded myself that students who are frustrated in school need to be in situations where they are seen as knowledgeable.

cognates. I also taught the students a self-assessment technique that helped them monitor their level of understanding and develop strategies for remembering new words. I chose about 10 words for every five pages of text for this kind of study. I made sure to continue to recycle vocabulary that occurred often in the text and that had not yet been mastered by the students. The students worked in buddy pairs (elbow pairs) for the activity. The buddy pairs had to assess how well they understood the vocabulary along three dimensions:

I Know It   I Think I Know It   I Don't Know It

- The students knew that if they checked *I Know It,* they would have to define the word for the rest of the class. This caveat prevented them from routinely checking the first column. This part of the activity took about 5 minutes. After completing the checks, the students took turns defining the words they knew. Next, we focused on words they thought they knew and words they did not know at all. At this point, I modeled sentences containing context clues, synonyms, or definitions to aid in comprehension of unknown words. I pantomimed words such as *frowned* and *muttering.* We searched for cognates in the Spanish language; Roberto was helpful in finding cognates because his Spanish was quite well developed. Finally, the students drew little pictures next to the unknown words to help them remember their meaning. The children enjoyed contributing ideas for pictures. The pictures on Maureen's vocabulary list, which is shown on page 121, indicate that she is capturing the general meaning of the target vocabulary.

- Assessment: The children's vocabulary self-assessment lists were very helpful to me in my own assessment of their work. I collected them and kept track of the vocabulary that children said they did not know. In this way, I could refer to these specific words when we met them again in the text, and I could recycle them onto new vocabulary lists. I was pleased to see that as we progressed through the text, the children were better able to incorporate the new vocabulary into some of their writing and could respond successfully to oral comprehension checks of the vocabulary we had studied.

Reading and Writing Development

The heart of a language arts unit is the development of reading and writing skills. This was especially true for my class of struggling readers and writers. I needed to increase the children's skills in those areas that would have the greatest academic impact for them. The unit on *The Most Beautiful Place in the World* had very specific goals geared to the kinds of reading skills my students would need in order to be successful in the fourth grade the following year. Most of these skills involved analytical thinking processes.

Some of the students whose reading skills were particularly low received additional, individualized, 30-minute reading sessions two or three times a week. At the beginning of the year, my co-teacher and I worked one-on-one with Bryan, Rudy, and Jorge in a computer-based program. These boys were interested in animals and the world of nature, so we chose a program called Curious Creatures (Taris & Taris, 1997). The software describes the characteristics of snakes, spiders, bats, wolves, and owls, and contains challenging academic language. The pictures and graphics are colorful and

Maureen's Vocabulary List

The Most Beautiful Place
pp 23-29

Name *Maureen*

Check the words in the correct column:

Vocabulary	I Know It	I Think I Know	I Don't Know It
1) muttering			✓
2) blackened			✓
3) tortillas	✓		
4) electricity	✓		
5) expensive	✓		
6) earned	✓		
7) frowned	✓		
8) resembles		✓	
9) empty	✓		
10) certainly		✓	

very motivating for 8- to 9-year-olds. The goals for these sessions were to increase reading time, expand decoding skills, and learn academic vocabulary and grammar. Bryan improved rapidly, moved out of the program within a few months, and began to read grade-level-appropriate books in his classroom and at home. At that point, Maureen took his place. The sessions with Maureen, Rudy, and Jorge continued until the end of the year. All of the students improved to the point at which they could understand the text on the computer. Elements critical to the progress of these students were the additional reading time, the one-on-one situation with a teacher, and the motivational nature of the software.

Goal 2, Standard 2 To use English to achieve academically in all content areas: Students will use English to obtain, process, construct, and provide subject matter information in spoken and written form.

Descriptors

- selecting, connecting, and explaining information in a text
- analyzing, inferring, and predicting from information in a text
- responding to questions in writing

Progress Indicators

- locate specific information in a text
- compare physical and cultural characteristics
- explain characters, scenes, and motivations in a text
- use the structure of a question to create a complete response in writing

---

During the first week of the unit, I had focused on activating the children's prior knowledge of Guatemala and developing their comprehension of geographic concepts and language. At this point, I wanted the children to think about the cultural differences that are described in the book. This was an attempt on my part to make a connection with the social studies concepts that are identified for third graders in my school district:

- People of similar cultural groups often live together in world communities.
- Families in world communities differ from place to place.
- Beliefs, customs, and traditions in world communities are learned from others and may differ from place to place. (Bedford Central School District, n.d., p. 11)

PROCEDURE

- We began Week 2 by reading a description of San Pablo, the fictional town described in the first three pages of *The Most Beautiful Place in the World* (Cameron, 1988). I showed pictures of typical South American towns, birds, foliage, and volcanoes. We then began a **visualization** of the town, and the students drew pictures of what they thought it looked like. Jorge's picture of San Pablo, which is shown on page 123, indicates that he clearly understood the major geographic features of the area: the three volcanoes, the lake, the hills with food crops and flowers growing on them, and the distinctive birds of the region.

- The next day, I drew a large Venn diagram on the easel chart and gave smaller copies to each student. On the chart, we listed ways in which San Pablo is different from the town in which the students live. Roberto's Venn diagram gives an example of what the students did (see p. 123).

Jorge's Picture of San Pablo

Roberto's Venn Diagram

San Pablo — Mount Kisco

San Pablo:
- Three huge dormant volcanoes
- a big lake
- Flowers and palm trees
- Corn Fields
- Coffe beans, garlic & onions
- Flocks of wild parrots

Mount Kisco:
- rolling hills
- a small pond at Leonard park
- deciduous trees
- Flowers in spring/summer
- birds in spring/summer

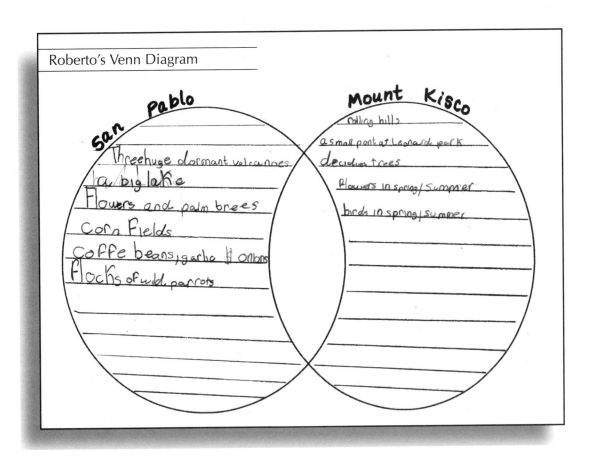

- The students used the diagram to describe the two towns orally, using compound comparison-and-contrast sentences. To ensure that the children would learn and use a variety of comparison/contrast signal words, I wrote words such as *but, however,* and *while* on the chart in red marker. The students chose from these words to create sentences of comparison and contrast, such as "San Pablo has three dormant volcanoes, but Mount Kisco has rolling hills" and "San Pablo has palm trees, while Mount Kisco has deciduous trees."

- The sentences in the Venn diagram contain vocabulary such as *dormant, deciduous,* and *rolling hills,* which are not in my students' oral vocabularies. I introduced these words to elaborate on the sentences they had created. The students were able to comprehend the new vocabulary using skills we had learned previously. For example, when Bryan commented that San Pablo had three volcanoes, I mentioned that the text said the volcanoes were *dormant* and wrote that word on the board. I told the students there was a word in Spanish like *dormant* and pantomimed sleeping. Roberto and Bryan immediately responded with *durmiendo.* We looked at both of those words on the blackboard and saw that they were almost the same. The students were then able to tell me that a *dormant* volcano is a sleeping volcano. The students each had two or three turns to create a sentence of comparison and contrast using the Venn diagram.

- Now I knew the students were ready to put the sentences into paragraph form, an exercise that we began the next day. The students were to write a descriptive paragraph about San Pablo that would accompany their pictures for a bulletin board display in the third-grade corridor. The class created a topic sentence for the paragraph we were going to write together. I wrote the topic sentence on my chart. This gave me an opportunity to model what the class had learned about paragraph writing. I decided to use a technique called **modeling thinking aloud.** For this technique, I told the class that I was going to pretend I was a third grader writing a paragraph about San Pablo. I was going to talk out loud about all the writing rules I needed to remember when writing the paragraph, such as capitalization, indention, and punctuation.

- After my demonstration, the students set to work to write in paragraph format what they had just practiced orally. The students used the Venn diagram to help them, and I kept the **key sentence frame** on the board to help Rudy, who was having difficulty getting started. The key sentence frame looked like this:

  San Pablo has _____, *but*   Mount Kisco has _____.

  San Pablo has _____, *while*   Mount Kisco has _____.

- After two class periods, all the students had completed their paragraphs. We used part of another class period to hang the finished work on the bulletin board.

- Throughout the daily reading of *The Most Beautiful Place in the World,* I found ways for the students to go back to the text to search for specific information. To do this, I asked a variety of comprehension questions after reading a section of the text, and asked the students to verify their answers by referring to the text. At first, I gave the students the page number on which to find the answer. I then taught the students to search for important reference words by skimming down a page of text with their fingers rather than rereading every word. Occasionally, students searched for information in buddy pairs.

Graphic organizers help ESOL students organize their writing in English. I collect graphic organizers that correspond to the four major text organizations emphasized in my elementary school, make sets of blank copies, and keep them on hand for short-term writing projects. The *Glossary of Techniques* at the end of this volume gives examples of the following graphic organizers: (a) simple listing (spider map), (b) compare and contrast (Venn diagram and double bubble), (c) chronology (time line and event map), and (d) cause and effect (flowchart).

- Answering questions in writing was a skill that I knew the students would need to master during third grade. I had observed that my students were unable to use the language of the question to help them compose a complete answer, so we had several minilessons on this skill, spending about 10 minutes a day for a few days in a row. I gave the students thin-line markers and a list of questions about the text. I asked them to underline the words in the questions that would be the beginning words in the answer. For example,

> Why does <u>Juan live with his grandmother</u>?
> Juan lives with his grandmother because . . .

- We practiced answering the questions orally using the underlined stems. Some of these transformations became difficult when I began to use "pastedown questions" that the classroom teachers had created for their units of study and photocopied for the students, usually with several questions on one page. The third-grade teachers asked their students to work independently to cut out one or two questions a day, paste them into their journals, and write a response under each question. The teachers felt that pastedown questions helped students create journal entries that were better organized and more complete. I wanted to use the same type of questions with my students, but I knew they would not be able to write answers independently without some language instruction. First, they needed oral practice sessions to help them learn the grammatical transformations required of some of these questions. For example, questions such as *What would you have done if you were Juan?* or *Would you try waking your grandmother or go to your mother's?* require transformations of pronouns and the rearrangement of the modal auxiliaries. We practiced some of these transformations orally before the students began to write in their notebooks.

- Assessment: Daily practice in writing answers in complete sentences gradually improved the students' ability to create sentences containing academic language and structures. I noticed from their pastedown sheets that, without my prompting, the students began to underline the parts of questions that were necessary to repeat in their answers. An example is shown on Roberto's notebook page (on page 126).

Roberto's Notebook Page

The Most Beautiful Place in the World p. 47

"When something's important, that's when you've got to say it!" my grandmother said. "You've got to stand up for yourself. It doesn't even matter if you lose. What matters is that you never stop trying to get what you really want. "Of course," she added, "I mean important things, not things like hot water and electricity."

Tell what Grandmother is trying to teach Juan.

What are the "important things" that **Juan** really wants?

What are the "important things" that **you** really want?

Grandmothe is trying to tech
Juan to stend up for his
sel

the impartant things that
Juan relly want is to go to
school

The important things that
I want is to be a police
officer.

• The students had opportunities to practice the language arts objectives for the unit within the context of social studies concepts. For example, the children read to determine the size of the family living in Juan's house and created diagrams to show the relationships among all the people in the family. From Francisco's family tree drawing, which is shown, we can see that he understood the relationships among all the people living in Juan's house.

• While the students were drawing their family trees, I talked with them about similarities in and differences between Juan's family and their own families.

Francisco's Family Tree

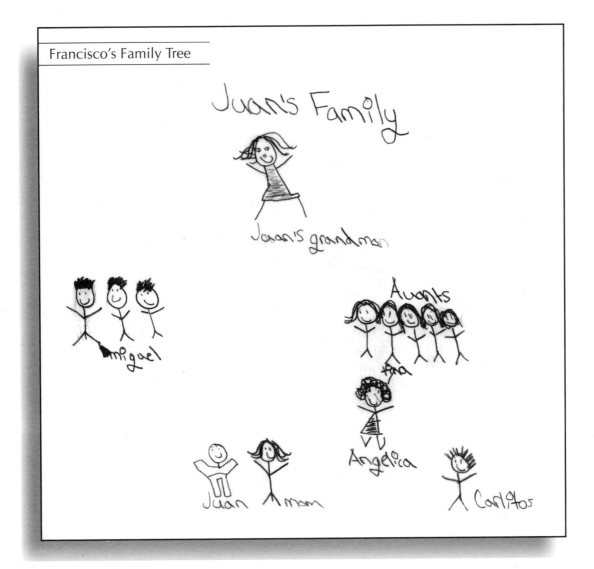

My students have large families in their native countries and often live with members of their extended families, but none of them had as large a family living in one house, as did Juan. They noted differences in their respective needs for electricity and plumbing as well as in family living conditions. These conversations helped me assess the students' understanding of social studies concepts related to culture.

- By the end of the unit, when we talked about the main theme of the book, most of the children had clearly understood that the theme was that love of family is an important element of life. When asked about the most beautiful place in their own world, all mentioned the importance of family in explaining their choices, as the student notebook pages shown on page 128 illustrate.

Behavior Management

One of my goals for this unit had been ongoing for the entire year. I wanted the students to feel secure enough in class to take the risks necessary to learn the language and content. In order to do that, I needed to establish routines and procedures that made the children feel comfortable, and I needed to be sure that their peers treated them respectfully. Verbal abuse was a possibility as several students were occasionally rowdy and

The most Beautiful place in the world to me is Spain because it has beach and there's no wers and big trees and my cousins are there and all my Family.

The Most Beautiful Place in the World to me is Panama because my Mom is there and my relatives and my grandparents and my cousins and my uncle.

The Most Beautiful place in the World to me is New york city because my aunt, uncle, and cousins. live dThere.

abusive on the playground and were management problems in their mainstream education classrooms.

I do not usually encounter management problems because I work with small groups of children, and small-group instruction tends to minimize the boredom and frustration that sometimes lead to unacceptable behavior in a larger class. But these youngsters had quite pronounced learning, social, and emotional needs. The family structures of some of the children were fractured. Learning disabilities frustrated three of the students to the point that they did not believe they could be successful readers and writers. At the beginning of the year, when I asked the children to write in their journals about what they wanted to learn that year, most of the children mentioned reading and writing. I felt that the affective goals for my students were very important ones, and I wanted to relate them to the language required for polite and appropriate behavior.

Goal 3, Standard 1 To use English in socially and culturally appropriate ways: Students will use the appropriate language variety, register, and genre according to audience, purpose, and setting.

Descriptor

- using the appropriate degree of formality with different audiences and settings

Progress Indicators

- interact with fellow students and adults in the formal setting of a classroom
- make polite requests
- demonstrate an understanding of how to apologize and express anger or impatience appropriately

---

Goal 3, Standard 2 To use English in socially and culturally appropriate ways: Students will use nonverbal communication appropriate to audience, purpose, and setting.

Descriptors

- demonstrating knowledge of acceptable nonverbal classroom behaviors
- using acceptable tone and volume in a classroom setting
- recognizing and adjusting behavior in response to nonverbal cues

Progress Indicators

- respond appropriately to a teacher's gesture or look
- obtain the teacher's attention in an appropriate manner
- use appropriate volume of voice in the classroom

PROCEDURE

Throughout the school year, I worked to develop strategies that modeled and encouraged good behavior and language, and discouraged poor examples. I believed that my students would adjust to the standards of the mainstream education class more quickly if they learned to conform to polite standards of language and behavior with adults and peers. Some of the strategies that proved to be most effective included the following:

- I modeled polite language when speaking to students.

- I reminded students of my expectations for behavior before beginning an activity, such as raising hands, using good listening skills, and using polite language. When students were not responding as expected, I reacted immediately. One method I used is called Stop the Action. I would stop all activity in the classroom by turning to face the offending students squarely, establishing eye contact, waiting long enough for the poor behavior to stop (5–7 seconds), saying "Thank you," and continuing the lesson. In this way, my students were alerted immediately to inappropriate behavior and were given an opportunity to discontinue the behavior before it accelerated.

- I tried to have "eyes in the back of my head." I monitored students constantly and made sure they were seated where I could see them. I walked around the classroom rather than staying in one place and quickly moved closer to any students who were not paying attention.

- I used checklists to record my students' progress in conforming to classroom behavior norms such as raising hands, listening to peers, and using polite language.

- I checked the comprehension of all students frequently throughout a lesson.

- I prepared my materials ahead of time so that I did not have to stop to find paper or markers in the middle of a lesson.

- I always spoke to students about poor behavior privately, never in front of classmates.

- I conferred with the classroom teachers frequently, sharing strategies for helping students manage themselves better in the mainstream classroom, establishing behavioral goals, and communicating with parents on a timely basis.

- I attempted to engage the students in meaningful and challenging activities and varied the activities often. The daily schedule shown on page 131 was typical of most of our classes.

Conclusion

It can be very frustrating to be limited to 50 minutes a day when working with very needy children. Pullout teaching, which requires that children be taught outside of their normal classroom environment, can also create problems for students and teachers. I could see, though, that the students I worked with in the unit on *The Most Beautiful Place in the World* (Cameron, 1988) were growing in both cognitive and affective ways. At the end of this 4-week unit, I was pleased to look back at the goals I had set a month earlier and note that my students had shown growth in every area. I was most pleased with the reading progress I observed in Bryan, Maureen, Rudy, and Jorge. I was impressed with the restraint that Roberto now used in class as he learned to control his impulsiveness. Cindy was better organized and completed more homework. Francisco's

Daily Schedule	
9:15–9:30	Morning song and greetings *Vocabulary Connections* work • Read nonfiction • Search for synonyms, context clues, cognates • Buddy teach • Take vocabulary test
9:30–10:00	*The Most Beautiful Place in the World* • Activate prior knowledge • Visualize and draw • Do vocabulary self-assessment • Buzz read • Answer comprehension questions • Search for specific information • Write answers to questions • Write summary paragraphs
10:00–10:10	• Summarize learning • Assess learning

classroom teacher and I agreed that he was ready to exit the program. At the end of the unit, as the class talked about their ideas for the most beautiful place in the world, I thought to myself that, for me, that day, my own classroom was the most beautiful place in the world.

RESOURCES AND REFERENCES

Bedford Central School District. (n.d.). *Social studies curriculum, Grade 3*. Mount Kisco, NY: Author.

Cameron, A. (1988). *The most beautiful place in the world*. New York: Random House.
Juan lives in the mountains of Guatemala, but his life is less than beautiful. His mother has abandoned him, and Juan works at shining shoes to earn money for his grandmother. His dream is to learn to read.

Taris, J. R., & Taris, L. J. (1997). Curious Creatures [CD-ROM]. North Billerica, MA: Curriculum Associates.
Curious Creatures is a set of five CD-ROMs that includes text and pictures of spiders, wolves, bats, owls, and snakes. There is an accompanying teacher's guide.

Popp, H. M., & Throop, S. (1994). *Literature enrichment activities for paperbacks*. Littleton, MA: Sundance. (Available from Sundance Publishers, PO Box 1326, Newtown Road, Littleton, MA 01460)
This is a two-page teacher's guide, part of the Literature Enrichment Activities for Paperbacks (LEAP) series for children's paperback novels.

Sharpe, D. (Exec. Ed.), & Sperry, J. (Project Ed.). (1997). *Vocabulary connections*. Austin, TX: Steck-Vaughn. (Available from Steck-Vaughn, PO Box 26015, Austin, TX 78755)
Vocabulary Connections is a series of soft-cover workbooks graded according to reading difficulty.

TESOL. (1997). *ESL standards for pre-K–12 students*. Alexandria, VA: Author.

TESOL. (in press). *Scenarios for ESL standards-based assessment*. Alexandria, VA: Author.

UNIT 6
Recycling

CARLYN SYVANEN

Introduction

The fifth graders in Mr. Moore's room showed that first-day-of-school mixture of confidence and shyness. The level of excitement was high, but the students' voices were quiet when I stepped into the class to greet students from last year and see who was new this year. Brenda called out from across the room, "Hi, Ms. Syvanen, can we be recycle this year?" Maria joined in, "Yes, please. Choose us, please." It was the beginning of my fourth year at this elementary school, and I smiled to think how much of a difference my students had made to the recycling program.

In my first year at the school, I had volunteered to be the recycling coordinator. It was my responsibility to pull together a committee made up of the custodian, the principal, and other interested staff to coordinate the school's recycling effort. In talking with other adults, I found that in the past at our school everything had been tried and nothing had worked. People would not commit themselves to meeting together or helping.

I decided to get students involved. We would try bottom-up rather than top-down organization. I taught ESL to Grades 4 and 5 in the school, and decided to designate one of my upper intermediate- or advanced-level ESL classes as the Recycling Team. It would be their responsibility to make presentations to other classes in the building about how important recycling was and about how to do it, to distribute recycling containers, and

---

Context

Grade level: Fifth grade

English proficiency levels: Upper intermediate–advanced

Native languages of students: Cambodian, Hmong, Oromo (an Ethiopian language), Portuguese, Russian, Spanish

Focus of instruction: Reading, writing, and speaking

Type of class: ESL through content, 30-minute daily pullout class

Length of unit: 6 weeks of intensive study; 1 year of school service

to collect recyclables once a week from the primary-grade classrooms and offices. The fourth- and fifth-grade classes were to carry their own recyclables to the bins. The ESL component of this program was so cleverly disguised that, at about the midpoint in the year, a Cambodian teaching assistant told me that the mother of one of my students had told him that her daughter had said that she was no longer in ESL; she thought that this was the recycling class.

Unit Overview

My goals for these students were to develop their skills in reading, writing, and speaking through meaningful work, as I believe that meaningful learning grows out of meaningful work. Recycling would provide them with the opportunity to read as they gathered information for their presentations. They would use writing to organize the information, write notices to inform others, and write letters to request information. They would use speaking to inform and persuade. On days when they picked up the recycled materials, they needed to know how to interrupt a class politely and how to respond to requests.

These upper intermediate- to advanced-level ESOL students were approaching

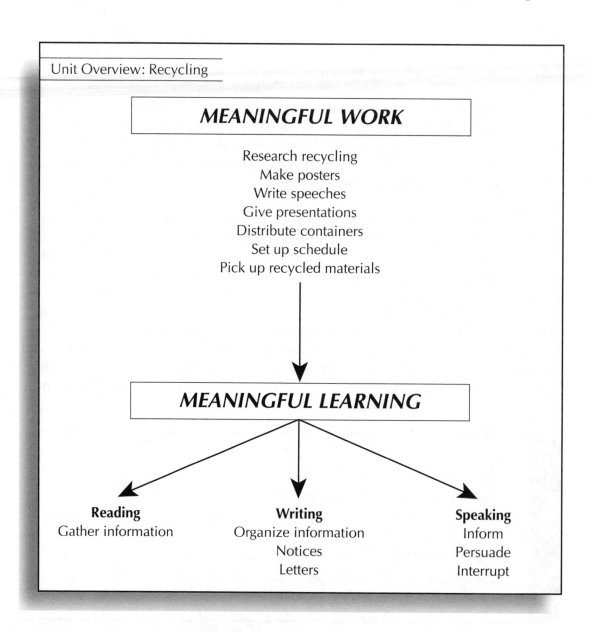

Unit Overview: Recycling

MEANINGFUL WORK

Research recycling
Make posters
Write speeches
Give presentations
Distribute containers
Set up schedule
Pick up recycled materials

MEANINGFUL LEARNING

Reading
Gather information

Writing
Organize information
Notices
Letters

Speaking
Inform
Persuade
Interrupt

grade-level expectations in fifth grade. Through discussions with their classroom teachers and from annual reading and writing assessments conducted in our district, I knew that some of the students were proficient readers but needed extra help in expressing themselves in writing. Others were proficient writers and could decode text fluently but were unsure of what they were reading. All needed to develop skill in speaking before an audience because of a new state requirement that all fifth-grade students pass a benchmark in speaking, which teachers were to document by scoring students' speeches throughout the year. Teachers were trained to score the speeches on ideas and content, organization, language, and delivery.

The unit on recycling occurred during the first 6 weeks of the school year. For the project, we researched the why and how of recycling, made posters, wrote short speeches, made presentations to the rest of the school, distributed recycling containers, set up a schedule, and made paper. For the rest of the year, we picked up recycled materials from the rest of the school on Fridays. The unit overview on page 134 shows the relationship of the recycling activities to student learning.

Standards

I had been teaching the recycling unit and having one of my ESL classes do recycling for 2 years before TESOL published *ESL Standards for Pre-K–12 Students* (1997). When I sat down to plan for the beginning of the school year, I was pleased to see how well the activities I had planned for this unit covered the three goals identified by TESOL that "reflect three overarching areas in which students need to develop competence in English: social language, academic language, and sociocultural knowledge" (p. 15). I realized that, in this unit, my students would be able to focus more on Goal 1 (social language) and Goal 3 (sociocultural knowledge) than usually occurs in my other ESL classes. Although the emphasis in this unit was on reading and writing, the unit also placed considerable emphasis on communicating in social settings and in socially and culturally appropriate ways.

After comparing my goals and unit activities with the ESL standards, I noticed areas that were a little weak in terms of how they addressed the standards. I then adjusted the unit so as to address goals and standards more thoroughly. For example, in previous years, we simply made paper, and that was that. After becoming familiar with the standards, I realized that I should integrate more academic activities, and I began to ask the students to write about the process of making paper. The standards were an affirmation of what I was doing in the classroom; they also served to nudge me closer to an ideal of teaching that I aspire to.

Activities

Introducing the Unit

To begin the unit, I asked the students to sort the contents of some randomly selected wastebaskets in order to discover independently how much recyclable material goes into the garbage. What I discovered was that they already knew a great deal about recycling. We then used the results of our research to make a large hallway bulletin board display to encourage more recycling.

Goal 2, Standard 1 **To use English to achieve academically in all content areas: Students will use English to interact in the classroom.**

Descriptors

- following oral and written directions, implicit and explicit
- participating in full-class, group, and pair discussions
- negotiating and managing interaction to accomplish tasks
- explaining actions

Progress Indicators

- use polite forms to negotiate and reach consensus
- take turns when speaking in a group
- modify a statement made by a peer

Goal 2, Standard 2 **To use English to achieve academically in all content areas: Students will use English to obtain, process, construct, and provide subject matter information in spoken and written form.**

Descriptors

- gathering information orally and in writing
- retelling information
- representing information visually and interpreting information presented visually

Progress Indicators

- construct a chart synthesizing information
- define, compare, and classify objects
- record observations
- construct a chart or other graphic showing data

PROCEDURE

- On the second day of class, I brought in the contents of three wastebaskets from different classrooms. I explained to the students that we were going to sort through the garbage to find out how much recyclable material and how much trash went into classroom wastebaskets.

- First, we weighed the full garbage bags. We then spread newspapers on the floor and dumped out the contents. "Ooh," "Ugh," and "I'm not touching that!" were soon replaced by "Look at all that good paper. Who threw that away?" Wearing rubber gloves, the students began to sort. I had provided the students with guidelines for recycling from the school district's recycling coordinator, with the intention that if we came across anything questionable, they could refer to it. As I listened to my students and watched them separate the trash from the recyclables, I found that they were quite knowledgeable about recycling and quite opinionated, too, as the following conversation excerpt illustrates. (In this unit, all names are pseudonyms except for Leranchona, Yuliya, Diego, Bumi, Salih, and Alla, which are used with permission.)

Bumi:	[picking out scraps of plastic laminating material] Where does this go?
Leranchona:	Plastic. Plastic you can't recycle.
Anna:	[holding up a stack of 2-inch white strips of paper] Someone can make good bookmarks out of this.
Jet:	This paper is new.
Yuliya:	Some people are too rich. That's why they throw it away.

- We then weighed the two piles. We found that we had 200 grams of trash and 1,200 grams of recyclables.

- We graphed the results of our study in a bar graph and decided to make a bulletin board to illustrate what we had found (see drawing below).

- The next day, we began the construction of the bulletin board. The students decided to call it "What We Found in the Wastebaskets." Through discussion, the students decided to do a three-dimensional display. They used crumpled papers from the recycling bin for a border. They made a

Drawing of Bulletin Board

wastebasket with crumpled paper and attached it to the display so that it stood out from the wall. They included two-dimensional representations of the trash and the recyclables, the scales, the graph, and a group account of what we had done and found out. Students suggested all the elements for the bulletin board, and I took on the role of layout advisor. One of the students typed up a group experience story to include on the bulletin board.

> Ms Syvanen said to us to look in the garbage and we did. We looked and divided it into parts of recyclables and trash.
> 1. We weighed the garbage first.
> 2. We put on rubber gloves.
> 3. We dumped the trash on the table.
> 4. We divided it into two bags, trash and recyclables.
> 5. We weighed the trash and the recyclables.
> 6. We found a lot more recyclables than trash in the wastebaskets.

Collecting Information

In order to collect information to present to the rest of the school, we needed to research the topic. We used a number of sources, including magazine articles, books, and videos.

Goal 2, Standard 2   To use English to achieve academically in all content areas: Students will use English to obtain, process, construct, and provide subject matter information in spoken and written form.

Descriptors

- comparing and contrasting information
- gathering information orally and in writing
- retelling information

Progress Indicators

- locate information appropriate to an assignment in text or reference materials
- research information on academic topics from multiple sources
- use contextual clues

PROCEDURE

- I located four videos on recycling that are made for children: *Recycling* (Mokin, 1985), *Recycle That Trash* (Pyramid Film Productions, 1990), *Recycling Is Fun* (Bullfrog Films, 1991), and *Recycling: It's Everybody's Job* (National Geographic Society, 1992). We watched the videos during the next 2 weeks of our project. After viewing each video, we discussed what we had learned about recycling, and added new information to a list we kept on chart paper. The four videos presented essentially the same information, but because of variations in how information was shared, different elements and facts were emphasized in each.

- Between viewing videos, we read articles and looked through books from the library. As students located new information, we added it to the chart, which, when completed, contained 10 reasons for recycling.

> **Why it is Important to Recycle:**
>
> Save trees from being cut down
> Trees make paper, cereal boxes, newspapers, and recycled paper can do that, too
> Helps animals
> Saves trees for birds, squirrels, owls, bugs, bears
> Keeping trash out of water helps fish
> Fish also need the shade of the trees to keep their water cooler
> Our land gets used up for landfills when garbage is not recycled
> We won't run out of steel and aluminum if we recycle cans
> Recycling uses less energy than making things from new
> It helps people to live in their houses when energy is saved

Creating a Presentation

The above activities took us into Week 3. It was now time to begin pulling the information together and preparing a presentation to share with the rest of the school.

Goal 2, Standard 2 **To use English to achieve academically in all content areas: Students will use English to obtain, process, construct, and provide subject matter information in spoken and written form.**

Descriptors

- persuading, arguing, negotiating, evaluating, and justifying
- retelling information
- selecting, connecting, and explaining information
- representing information visually and interpreting information presented visually

Progress Indicators

- take a position and support it orally or in writing
- construct a chart synthesizing information

Goal 3, Standard 1   To use English in socially and culturally appropriate ways: Students will use the appropriate language variety, register, and genre according to audience, purpose, and setting.

Descriptors

- using the appropriate degree of formality with different audiences and settings
- using a variety of writing styles appropriate for different audiences, purposes, and settings

Progress Indicator

- prepare a short persuasive presentation for different audiences

PROCEDURE

- On Day 1, we reviewed all the information we had gathered and added new items to the chart.

- On Days 2–5, each student selected one of the issues listed on the chart as a focus for the group presentation that would be taken to other classes. They were to draw a poster and write a speech about their selected topic. The students worked individually or in pairs; students who were too shy to present on their topics alone worked with a partner.

> Over the years, I have found that students who are the most shy usually volunteer to do more of the talking after the first couple of presentations. I learned that it is best to allow students to work with a partner, if they feel the need to, in order to gain confidence.

- As the students revised their speeches, I drew their attention to those elements of language that make listening and understanding easier. These conversations with the students seemed to help them think through what they wanted and needed to say, and then write more clearly and effectively. As the following example shows, Anna did not incorporate my suggestions verbatim; instead, she integrated some of what we talked about, but did so in her own way, in her own voice.

Anna: [handing me her paper] Here, Ms. Syvanen, I'm done.

I read Anna's first draft.

Anna's First Draft

Help Animals by recycle saves trees for birds, squirrels, owls, bugs, and bears, and many more animals that can live in the wood because when you not recycle you make animals died by cutting down trees. If you recycle you will save tree and animals off died. when we recycle we save the thing in the wood. by Anna

Teacher: [reading the paper] This is very good. You have all the information here. I think there are some words that you can add, to make it easier to remember this much information.

[As I talk with Anna about her paper, other students are writing their first drafts or finishing up their posters; they pause in their work to listen to our conversation.]

Teacher: "Help Animals by recycling" would work as a title. There are some little words you can use to start the first sentence that will tie your ideas together. "When we recycle we save trees for . . . ." You won't need *because* now, and you can start the next sentence, which will tell what happens when we don't recycle. In English, we say *save animals from dying,* not *of died.* Now, what thing in the woods are you talking about?

Anna: Creatures?

Teacher: Good word. People will get a better picture of what you mean when you use the word *creatures.*

Anna's Final Draft

Help Animals

When we recycle we save trees for birds, squirrels, owls, bugs, bears and many more animals that live in the woods. When we don't recycle we make animals die by cutting down more tree. If you recycle we save the woods and creatures that live in the woods. when we recycle we can make new papers. If we don't recycle we will make the woods look ugly. If we recycle we will make the world beautiful.

Several of the students drew pictures on both sides of the paper (two-sided pictures) to illustrate the negative and positive effects of recycling. Jet labeled his poster, "If we stop recycle the world will be trash . . . . But if we recycle everything will be ok." Yuliya's two-sided picture, which is shown on page 142, illustrates what happens when slopes are deforested, ponds and lakes lose their shade, and water becomes too hot for fish.

- When Yuliya, the first person to draw a two-sided picture, read her first draft to me, I mentioned that she could put instructions to herself in parentheses so that she would know what to do when making her presentation and would not accidentally read the instructions aloud. I had noticed that students often read every word they had written when making an oral presentation, and this was an attempt to help them focus on what needed to be said. As I read the other students' papers, I noticed that all students who had two-sided pictures also included directions to themselves in parentheses.

- On Day 6, when the students had completed their posters and speeches, they began rehearsing their presentations. At first, they decided to make their presentations in the order that their topics appeared on the chart. However, I asked them to be critical listeners, and think about what they were saying and how it fit in with what others were saying. After the first rehearsal, they agreed to rearrange speakers because the items on the list were not in a logical order. The group decided on the following order: Jet

Yuliya's Two-Sided Picture

Juvenato's Poster

opened the presentation, as he had written a speech that made a good introductory paragraph. Anna, Alla, and Yuliya followed with speeches about the benefits to animals and fish of recycling. Diego, who emphasized saving land from landfills, followed. Then Juvenato and Leranchona spoke separately about saving natural resources; Juvenato's poster (above) shows a picture of two tough-looking guys urging people to recycle their cans.

Leranchona talked about how recycling uses less energy, as did Bumi. Salih was new to the group and missed the videos and articles; he told about what should go into the recycling bins in the classrooms and how all the kids in school needed to take responsibility for recycling.

Throughout the rehearsal process, the students were revising and editing their speeches. As Anna was reading her speech, she repeatedly stumbled when she came to the line, "When you recycle we save the woods and creatures . . . ." Suddenly she said, "I can't read this because it sounds funny." She paused and then continued: "I know what's wrong. It should be, 'When we recycle we save the . . . .'" She laughed, and then added, "You recycle so we save." Leranchona also found the rehearsal process helpful in refining her writing. She was reading her speech aloud: "Recycling uses less energy than making things from new. When you recycle aluminum cans they will be broken up into little pieces then they will be melted. It takes less energy to make old glass into new glass. The factory workers take sand to make glass. They take wood to make paper." Once she had finished reading, she looked up thoughtfully and said, "That's not a real ending. I have to say something else to make it sound like the

Leranchona's Poster

end." She then added, "When they make paper from old paper it takes less energy than making paper from wood." The poster that Leranchona drew to accompany her speech is shown above.

It became clear that we needed to talk about effective presentation strategies. We focused on issues such as speaking up, not holding posters in front of our faces, and speaking more slowly.

Preparing Written and Verbal Communications

Throughout the project, the students had opportunities to work on communication skills beyond the more formal area of making speeches. As part of the recycling unit, they had to politely interrupt classes, take requests, write notes, and request supplies.

PROCEDURE

- When the students first began working on their posters, two students made a blank schedule with a note to teachers asking them to sign up for a convenient time for the group to come to their classroom to make the recycling presentation.

- Later, the students who had finished making their posters and preparing their speeches wrote to teachers reminding them of the time and day we would visit their classes. I worked with these students to achieve the appropriate tone for reminder notes. The task of writing the notes was relatively simple, but I was able to teach them several shortcuts on the computer, such as copying the note and inserting different times,

Goal 1, Standard 1 To use English to communicate in social settings: Students will use English to participate in social interactions.

Descriptors

- sharing and requesting information
- conducting transactions

Progress Indicators

- engage listeners' attention
- elicit information and ask clarification questions
- give and ask for permission

Goal 3, Standard 3 To use English in socially and culturally appropriate ways: Students will use appropriate learning strategies to extend their sociolinguistic and sociocultural competence.

Descriptor

- rehearsing variations of language use in different social and academic situations

Progress Indicator

- rehearse ways of politely interrupting when entering a classroom

dates, and teachers' names. When they had completed the notes, the students went to the office and put the notes in teachers' boxes.

- On days when we picked up recyclables, the students had to go into classrooms to pick up the recycling bags while class was in session. On the first day that we picked up these bags, we spent a few minutes rehearsing polite ways to interrupt a class. We settled on "Excuse us, may we pick up the recycling now?" During the course of the year, we talked about other ways to interrupt politely. Generally speaking, the students developed a wider range of useful polite interruption phrases and came to realize that, as Juvenato said, "It depends on what they say to us!"

- As part of the recycling activities, the students often had to request supplies as well as respond to requests from teachers for items such as new recycling bags and bins. We took a few minutes to rehearse these situations so the students would have the phrases and vocabulary to help them communicate effectively. The format of these sessions was often that I asked the students what they would say in a given situation. After they volunteered possibilities, I then suggested more specific words or phrases to help make their meaning clearer. For example, students often overused *thing* and *stuff,* and we talked about the importance of using the appropriate names for objects.

Making Paper

The National Geographic Society's 1992 video, *Recycling Is Everybody's Job,* shows students in a classroom making paper out of scrap paper. As soon as the students saw this video, they asked if we could make paper, too. I thought this would be a good opportunity for us to ask some *what if* questions and experiment to find answers.

Goal 2, Standard 2 **To use English to achieve academically in all content areas: Students will use English to obtain, process, construct, and provide subject matter information in spoken and written form.**

Descriptors

- comparing and contrasting information
- selecting, connecting, and explaining information
- representing information visually and interpreting information presented visually

Progress Indicators

- construct a chart synthesizing information
- record observations
- ask questions and be able to predict different answers according to materials used

---

Procedure

- The basic recipe for making paper requires water and used paper torn into little pieces. This is put in the blender until it is pulpy. It is then poured on a screen, drained, and dried. As I was demonstrating the process, students started asking questions: "What if you use different colors?" "What if you use only newspaper?" "What if . . . ?" Because I had only one blender in the room, students had to take turns. While waiting for their turns, they generated questions, predicted results, and collected materials. Their questions ranged from "What happens when we use paper bags?" to "What happens if we use newsprint?" Sometimes their predictions were accurate, but at other times they were logical but not accurate. For example, they predicted that the print on newsprint would be leached out, whereas in practice, the letters transferred to the recycled paper.

- Over the course of 2 days, the students made a range of papers. Through these experiments with mixing different kinds of paper, we found that, by varying what was in the mixtures, we could make paper of different colors and textures.

- When the paper was dry and had been pressed, we looked at the resulting paper through loupes (small, single magnifying lenses that fit close to the eye). The students then wrote about what their paper looked like through the loupe: "My paper looks like little mountains." "It looks like fur on the edges." "There are little pieces of letters in my paper."

- As a culminating project for the paper-making activity, we made a bulletin board display about making paper. The students drew pictures of each step in the process and wrote descriptions. Because each student had used a different mixture and ended up with a different product, each also wrote what mixture was used in their paper and what it looked like through the loupe.

- As noted, Oregon fifth-grade students must make speeches as part of their grade-level benchmark assessment. Some of the students in this group used the information from the bulletin board for an expository speech that they delivered in their mainstream classrooms.

Making Presentations on Recycling to Other Classes

Once the students had practiced their presentations, they were ready to take them into other classrooms.

Goal 3, Standard 1 To use English in socially and culturally appropriate ways: Students will use the appropriate language variety, register, and genre according to audience, purpose, and setting.

Descriptor

- using the appropriate degree of formality with different audiences and settings

Progress Indicator

- deliver a short persuasive presentation to different audiences

Goal 3, Standard 2 To use English in socially and culturally appropriate ways: Students will use nonverbal communication appropriate to audience, purpose, and setting.

Descriptor

- demonstrating knowledge of acceptable nonverbal classroom behaviors

Progress Indicators

- maintain appropriate level of eye contact with audience while giving an oral presentation

- use appropriate gestures when referring to visuals in an oral presentation

PROCEDURE

- Over the course of 6 school days, the students took their presentation to 24 classrooms, where they showed their posters and made brief speeches. They made four speeches in each of six 30-minute periods. All the presentations were scheduled during the half hour we met daily.

- The students also took the recycling containers with them to the classrooms and demonstrated what should go into recycling and what should go into the trash.

- In the classes, they asked if anyone had any questions and answered those that were closest to their topics.

- Our school has a Spanish/English dual-language program. In the Spanish language classrooms, Diego, the Spanish-speaking member of the team, explained the process in Spanish. He had written the shortest speech of the group and had been the most hesitant to speak in front of the classes, but when he was called upon to translate for the Spanish classes, he stepped in readily and became an enthusiastic member of our team.

Conclusion

The degree to which this unit was successful was reflected in greatly increased awareness of recycling throughout the school in the weeks after the students made their presentations; in fact, the students noticed that they were picking up more recyclables each week. At the end of the in-class presentations, audience members applauded energetically and commented favorably on the group members' posters. Classroom teachers always commented on how much they liked the students' talking to peers about recycling, as it was a big support for the teachers' own efforts to recycle. The students also gained a lot of confidence from speaking in front of others. At first, they were very hesitant to go into classes, but by the end they were excited and motivated. The following year, they were anxious to repeat the experience, as Brenda's comment, quoted at the beginning of this unit, illustrates: "Hi, Ms. Syvanen, can we be recycle this year?"

RESOURCES

Books for Children and Young Adults

Amos, J. (1995). *Waste and recycling*. Austin, TX: Raintree Steck-Vaughn.
  The text, drawings, and photos provide clear, simple messages about the problems of having too much waste. There is a brief explanation of recycling.

Brooks, F. (1991). *Protecting trees and forests*. New York: Scholastic.
  This book, from the series Usborne Conservation Guides, *provides specific information on threats to the forests of the world. Recycling paper is only one of many solutions described.*

Davis, W. (1995). *From tree to paper*. New York: Scholastic.
  This photo essay, accompanied by a simple text, shows the process of making paper.

The Earth Works Group. (1989). *50 simple things you can do to save the earth*. Berkeley, CA: Earthworks Press.
  The sections on recycling are full of facts that help students understand larger concepts and show how individuals can make a difference to the preservation of the environment.

James, B. (1990). *Waste and recycling*. Austin, TX: Steck-Vaughn.
  The text and concepts in this book are more complex than the other materials we used, but the photographs are very dramatic, and the graphics clearly illustrate concepts that were difficult for my students.

Kalbacken, J., & Lepthien, E. U. (1991). *A new true book: Recycling.* Chicago: Children's Press.
Concepts and facts surrounding the issues of too much trash and the importance of recycling are presented simply and with pictures that clearly illustrate the points.

Mattson, M. (1993). *Scholastic environmental atlas of the United States.* New York: Scholastic.
This atlas provides interesting facts about environmental features around the United States.

Tinzmann, M. (1990). *Too much trash?* Columbus, OH: Zaner-Bloser.
This 25-page, workbook-style paperback, part of the series Breakthroughs: Strategies for Thinking, by Beau Fly Jones, poses problems and provides frameworks for problem solving.

Videos and Films

Bullfrog Films (Producer). (1991). *Recycling is fun* [Video]. (Available from Bullfrog Films, Oley, PA 19547; telephone 1-800-543-3764)
This video is recommended for Grades K–5. It shows young people entertaining themselves as they participate in local recycling programs. It demonstrates why the 3 Rs (reduce, recycle, and reuse) are necessary, that recycling activities can be enjoyable, and that young people can help save the environment.

Mokin, A. (Producer). (1985). *Recycling* [Film]. (Available from Arthur Mokin Productions, 2900 McBride Lane, Santa Rosa, CA 95401)
This 16-mm film is recommended for Grades 3–8. It points out that solid waste disposal sites are rapidly becoming filled and proposes recycling as a partial solution. The depiction of the industrial processes by which materials such as old newspapers, glass bottles, and metal cans are made into new products is very impressive.

National Geographic Society (Producer). (1992). *Recycling is everybody's job* [Video]. (Available from National Geographic Society, 1145 17th Street NW, Washington, DC 20036-4688; telephone 1-800-857-7669)
This video is recommended for Grades 4–5. It follows a class recycling project in which students separate trash and learn why recycling is the most logical answer to the garbage problem.

Pyramid Film Productions (Producer). (1990). *Recycle that trash* [Video]. (Available from Pyramid Film Productions, 2801 Colorada Avenue, Santa Monica, CA 90404)
This video is recommended for Grades K–5. A teacher and her students visit landfills, transfer stations, and recycling centers. They suggest ways for students to apply what they learn in the classroom by implementing recycling programs at home.

Resources for Teachers

Department of Environmental Quality. (1992). *Rethinking recycling: An Oregon waste reduction curriculum.* Portland, OR: Author.
This resource guide provides information to make the teacher an expert on recycling. A packet of teaching materials, including units and lesson plans about all aspects of recycling, accompanies the guide. It is also appropriate for teachers who do not live or work in Oregon.

TESOL. (1997). *ESL standards for pre-K–12 students.* Alexandria, VA: Author.

Glossary of Techniques

Procedures often vary somewhat from teacher to teacher. The following descriptions represent one widely accepted variant, but implementation may change depending on the teacher and the context.

Author's chair: An occasion for students to read their writing aloud to the class (or a group of students and the teacher). The students and teacher then respond to the writing.

- Encourage students to share their writing in author's chair as one part of the process of becoming a better writer. Students should not be forced to share their writing. Many students who are initially shy about sharing their writing in author's chair gain confidence after responding to their peers' writing.

- Discuss good listening techniques, such as not talking to or making faces at a neighbor and keeping eyes on the reader or on a spot in the room, such as the rug, that will not be distracting.

- Set up a scheduled time for author's chair; this might be 20 minutes daily at the end of writers' workshop.

- Identify a special chair or a place on the rug where the writer sits so authors are at the center of attention.

- Demonstrate, teach, and expect positive but critical response. Invite students to comment first on what is good before asking the author questions that clarify content or making suggestions for how to improve the writing. Encourage students to discuss the content as well as the style of the writing.

- Have authors take written notes of the audience members' comments so they may later revise their writing to make it better.

Dialogue journal: A two-way journal in which a teacher and student, or two students, conduct a conversation on paper.

- Make sure all students have notebooks or folders for their dialogue journal entries.

- Explain the purpose of the dialogue journals, and tell students that, although you will read and respond to entries, you will not correct or grade them. Also explain that before they write their entries, they should respond to what you have written.

- Discuss possible content for their entries; some teachers invite students to write about any topics that interest them, whereas others focus dialogue journals on a particular subject (e.g., literature or mathematics).

- Set up a schedule for journal writing. The writing may be done during class or at home, with the journals turned in on a particular day. Some teachers (such as Jim Hughes, who wrote Unit 2 in this volume) allow time in class each day for students to write in their dialogue journals and then respond to them all before the next day's class. Sometimes it is difficult for a teacher to respond on a daily basis to every child's entry, particularly when students are older and write longer entries. In these cases, it is helpful to stagger the turning in of journals or reduce the frequency with which students write entries.

- Respond to students' entries in a natural, authentic, and meaningful way, as if carrying on a conversation. For example, you might comment on how something the student has written is similar to an experience you have had. Try not to dominate or control the interaction. Although many advocates of dialogue journals encourage teachers not to use directives or questions in their responses, authentic response may sometimes lend itself to doing just that. For example, you might need to ask a question about something that is unclear or incomplete or urge a student to *please* complete an entry, as you want to know more!

- Although teachers do not correct students' dialogue journal entries, it is appropriate to model the correct form in responses. For example, if a student misspells a word, you might use the correct spelling in the response.

Elbow buddies (sometimes referred to as **buddy pairs**): An opportunity for students to work with a peer in solving a problem, generating answers to a question, discussing an issue, or reflecting on a process. The activity lasts just a few minutes.

- Have the students each pair up with the child seated next to one of their elbows.

- Give each pair a question to answer, a problem to solve, an issue to discuss, or a process to reflect on.

Graphic organizers: Visual representations of ideas and the relationships among them. They can be used before, during, and after reading to help students process, understand, and retain information, and to monitor comprehension. They can also help students organize their writing. Graphic organizers referred to in this volume include

- spider map
- double bubble
- Venn diagram
- time line
- event map
- flowchart

Examples of each of these are shown on pages 156–160.

Guided reading: An approach to teaching reading that bridges shared and independent reading. Students read independently after the teacher has prepared them for the reading. (For more information, see Fountas & Pinnell, 1996.)

- Introduce a picture book (either fiction or nonfiction) by drawing out the students' background knowledge. Ask the students to make predictions about the content of the book based on the front cover.

- With the students, "walk through" the book page by page, again making predictions and connecting content to their background knowledge. At this time, introduce key vocabulary and concepts.

- Before students begin to read the text independently, set a purpose for the reading. The purpose may be related to content (e.g., to find out why the main character made a certain decision) or to a reading strategy that students need to learn or practice (e.g., using headings when reading; in this case, you might ask students to make predictions based on headings and then read the text under the headings to confirm or disconfirm their predictions).

- Ask the students to read independently, aloud or silently. While they are reading, work with selected individual students, who read aloud to you, and help them with reading strategies you have selected based on their needs. During this time, you might keep anecdotal records of any problems or successes experienced by the student.

- When the children have finished reading independently, have them come back together with you and discuss the specific strategy targeted for that reading session.

- Use the information gained during this discussion and in individual sessions with students to plan future lessons.

Key sentence frame: A technique that is used to help emergent writers develop syntactically correct sentences.

- Write a sample sentence on the board.

- Ask the students to use these sentences to generate others that fit the same pattern.

K-W-L chart: A technique that uses brainstorming to determine what students already know about a topic, what they want to learn about it, and, afterward, what they actually did learn. It is a useful tool for assessing prior knowledge, planning instruction, and summarizing learning.

- When a topic is introduced, have the students brainstorm what they know already about the topic. This is listed in the *Know* (*K*) column. Sometimes teachers immerse students in a topic for a couple of days before activating this column.

- Then have the students brainstorm what they would like to know about the topic, and list this in the *Want to Know* (*W*) column. Some teachers also ask students to brainstorm how they might find answers to their questions, thus creating a list of potential resources.

- If you wish, add a third column for what students have *Learned* (*L*), which is completed at the end of the unit and summarizes what students have learned.

Modeling thinking aloud: A technique used by teachers to teach how to think about a process, such as writing an essay, editing one's writing, conducting library research, or making a sandwich.

- Think aloud while demonstrating the process.
- Through thinking aloud, show how you self-monitor, predict, confirm, and plan.

Reading circles: Reading groups in which students select the book they will read from a limited selection offered by the teacher.

- Group students according to the book they choose.
- Meet with the book groups regularly to discuss the part of the book that they have read since the previous discussion.
- When they are not meeting with you, have the students work either alone or in pairs on book-related activities, such as journal entries or cognitive mapping activities.
- Teach minilessons as needed to the entire class.

Reciprocal teaching: A technique for strengthening reading comprehension in which students are taught four strategies—predicting, clarifying, summarizing, and questioning—in the hope that they will then incorporate the strategies that good readers use in their independent reading.

- While a group reads a selection together, they engage aloud in these four strategies to better comprehend the text.
- Students learn to lead this process and teach each other.

Running record: A system of notations for recording the miscues (e.g., omissions, substitutions, self-corrections) that a child makes while reading aloud. Later, the teacher determines which of the language cueing systems (e.g., graphophonic, syntactic, semantic) the child is probably tapping into when making miscues or self-correcting. (For more information, see Clay, 1993.)

- As the student reads aloud, record correctly read words with a check mark, and use a system of abbreviations to indicate common miscues (e.g., substitutions, omissions, reversals).
- Optionally, in a separate section note the child's strengths, such as reading a particularly difficult word or one the child previously miscued.
- Use the records to plan individual instruction or focused small-group or class lessons.

Ticket to leave: A summarizing technique used by teachers at the end of a class to determine if students know what has been taught during that class.

- At the end of the class period, ask questions based on what has been taught.

- Tell the students that they must answer a question correctly, either orally or in writing, in order to leave the classroom.

Venn diagram: A graphic organizer used to compare and contrast. (See the example of a Venn diagram at the end of this section.)

- Discuss the subjects that you want students to compare and contrast.

- Guide the students to write information that applies to both subjects in the overlapping section of the two circles.

- Ask the students to write information that applies to only one of the subjects in one or the other of the nonoverlapping sections of the circles.

Visualization: A technique for helping students either prepare for a new topic or process information that has already been introduced.

- Tell the students to close their eyes and visualize a scene or event that they have experienced, read about, or studied.

- To help students visualize more vividly, read a script quietly or ask specific questions during the visualization time. Turning off the lights or playing appropriate music can also be helpful.

- After the students have visualized for a few minutes, ask them to talk briefly with a partner or to draw or write about their visualizations.

- If you wish, invite students to share their visualizations with the larger group.

REFERENCES

Clay, M. (1993). *An observation survey of early literacy achievement.* Portsmouth, NH: Heinemann.

Fountas, I. C., & Pinnell, G. S. (1996). *Guided reading: Good first teaching for all children.* Portsmouth, NH: Heinemann.

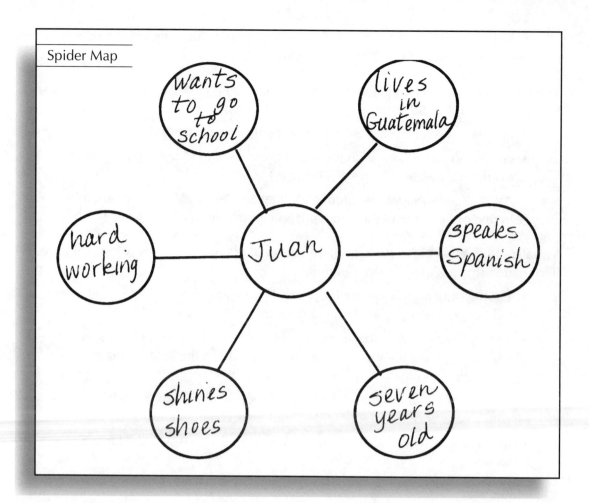

Spider Map

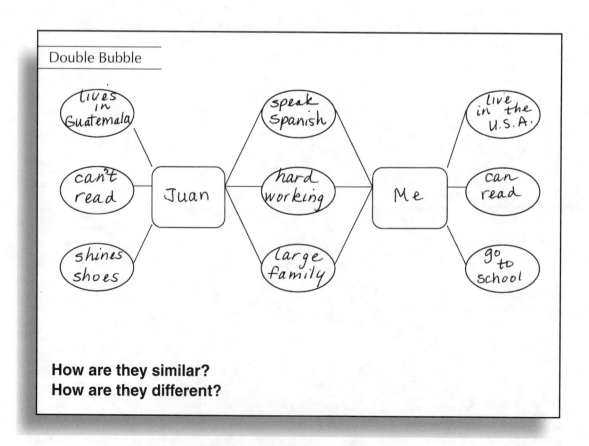

Double Bubble

How are they similar?
How are they different?

Venn Diagram: "The Three Little Pigs" and "The Three Bears"

Three Little Pigs

3 pigs build houses

Wolf visits the houses

Wolf blows down two
houses

Wolf is killed by the pigs

**3
characters
3
events
an intruder**

**characters get
rid of intruder
& live happily
ever after**

The Three Bears

3 bears live in a house

Goldilocks visits the house

Goldilocks eats porridge
& breaks a chair

Goldilocks is frightened by
the bears & leaves

JUAN PONCE DE LEON

1474   was born in _____

1493   sailed with_____
on a voyage to
America.

settled in _____.

1508   explored Puerto Rico
and found _____there.

conquered _____
& became first governor.

1513

searched for the Fountain
of _____in southern
_____.

1521   was killed in_____.

Event Map

Juan was abandoned by his father and mother.

1

Juan lived with his grandmother and shined shoes.

2

Juan taught himself to read and do math.

3

Juan was permitted to attend school.

4

What is the sequence of events?

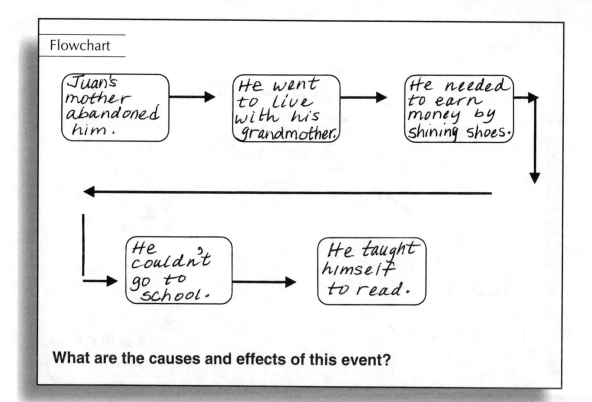

Flowchart

Juan's mother abandoned him. → He went to live with his grandmother. → He needed to earn money by shining shoes.

He couldn't go to school. → He taught himself to read.

What are the causes and effects of this event?

About the Editors and Writers

Sue DeFabbia is an itinerant ESL teacher in an urban school district in Rochester, New York, where she teaches in two schools, a K–6 elementary school and a 6–8 middle school. She also has taught adult ESOL students in college and adult education programs. She was first introduced to ESL teaching in the late 1980s, when she was a volunteer in Nicaragua.

Jim Hughes is a third-grade teacher in an urban school district in San Pablo, California, where he works with students from diverse backgrounds, many of them nonnative English speakers. He is a writer as well as a teacher. He recently won a district teaching excellence award.

Suzanne Irujo, editor of this series, has taught ESL at all grade levels and spent many years teaching methodology and language acquisition courses and supervising ESL student teachers at Boston University. Her BA is in Spanish, her EdM is in bilingual education, and her EdD is in second language acquisition. She is semiretired, dividing her time between consulting on and editing ESL-related projects and enjoying the New Hampshire woods.

Linda New Levine was, when she wrote this unit, a pullout ESL teacher in Mt. Kisco, a suburban school district about one hour's drive north of New York City. She has taught at Teachers College, Columbia University, for more than 15 years, is her district's staff development facilitator, and is a consultant. She has served as chair of TESOL's ESOL in Elementary Education Interest Section and has edited its newsletter.

Katharine Davies Samway, editor of this volume, is a professor of education in the Department of Teacher Education at San José State University, in California. She has been an ESL teacher, teacher educator, and researcher for more than 20 years. She has served as chair of TESOL's ESOL in Elementary Education Interest Section, as editor of its newsletter, and as associate editor of *TESOL Journal*.

Carlyn Syvanen is an ESL teacher in a large, very diverse elementary school in an urban school district in Portland, Oregon. She has been a teacher or administrator for many years, mostly in the United States but also abroad. She served as chair of TESOL's ESOL in Elementary Education Interest Section and coedited its newsletter.

Dorothy Taylor was a pullout ESL teacher in an elementary school in Fairfax County, Virginia, when she wrote the unit in this volume. She has been teaching ESL for about 20 years on the East Coast of the United States (Maryland, Virginia, western New York, and Massachusetts) and has taught both children and adults. She was the coeditor of "Tips from the Classroom" in *TESOL Journal* for 5 years.

Users' Guide

Volume and Unit

Grade Levels	Pre-K–2						3–5						6–8						9–12					
	1	2	3	4	5	6	1	2	3	4	5	6	1	2	3	4	5	6	1	2	3	4	5	6
Pre-K	X																							
Kindergarten		X	X																					
Grade 1			X	X																				
Grade 2			X	X	X	X																		
Grade 3			X					X		X	X													
Grade 4							X		X	X														
Grade 5							X				X									X				
Grade 6													X	X		X	X			X				
Grade 7															X		X	X		X				
Grade 8																X	X	X		X				
Grade 9																			X	X	X		X	X
Grade 10																			X	X	X		X	X
Grade 11																			X	X	X	X	X	X
Grade 12																			X	X		X	X	X

Language Proficiency Levels	Pre-K–2						3–5						6–8						9–12					
	1	2	3	4	5	6	1	2	3	4	5	6	1	2	3	4	5	6	1	2	3	4	5	6
Beginning	X	X	X	X	X			X	X				X	X	X		X			X				X
Intermediate	X	X		X	X	X	X	X		X	X	X	X	X	X	X	X	X	X	X	X	X	X	X
Advanced	X	X			X	X	X				X		X	X		X	X		X	X				X
Native Speaker	X	X			X	X	X							X										

Program Models	Pre-K–2						3–5						6–8						9–12					
	1	2	3	4	5	6	1	2	3	4	5	6	1	2	3	4	5	6	1	2	3	4	5	6
Pull-out ESL[1]			X	X			X	X	X	X	X	X												
Departmentalized ESL[2]							X								X	X						X	X	
Intensive English[3]																				X				
Sheltered English[4]																X	X		X					X
Inclusion/Push-in ESL[5]		X				X																		
Team Teaching[6]															X						X			
Mainstream Class[7]	X			X			X						X											

Language and Content Areas	Pre-K–2						3–5						6–8						9–12					
	1	2	3	4	5	6	1	2	3	4	5	6	1	2	3	4	5	6	1	2	3	4	5	6
Basic Academic Skills	X	X	X	X																				
Listening and Speaking	X	X	X	X	X	X	X	X	X	X	X	X	X	X	X	X	X	X	X	X	X	X	X	X
Reading		X		X	X	X	X	X	X	X	X	X	X			X	X	X					X	X
Writing			X	X	X			X	X	X	X	X			X	X	X	X	X	X	X	X	X	X
Social Studies			X				X	X	X	X	X	X				X			X					X
Science		X		X								X	X	X		X				X				
Mathematics		X		X								X	X							X				

Standards	Pre-K–2						3–5						6–8						9–12					
	1	2	3	4	5	6	1	2	3	4	5	6	1	2	3	4	5	6	1	2	3	4	5	6
Goal 1, Standard 1	X	X		X	X	X	X		X		X		X		X		X		X					X
Goal 1, Standard 2	X	X	X		X	X			X				X			X	X		X	X				
Goal 1, Standard 3	X	X		X	X	X	X	X							X							X	X	X
Goal 2, Standard 1	X	X	X	X	X	X	X		X	X	X	X		X	X	X	X	X				X	X	X
Goal 2, Standard 2	X	X	X	X	X	X	X	X	X	X	X	X	X	X	X	X	X	X	X	X	X	X	X	X
Goal 2, Standard 3	X		X	X	X	X	X		X	X	X		X	X	X		X	X	X	X	X	X	X	X
Goal 3, Standard 1			X	X	X	X	X			X	X	X		X	X	X			X	X	X			X
Goal 3, Standard 2				X	X											X	X		X					X
Goal 3, Standard 3		X		X	X								X	X					X					

[1] ESOL students spend most of their time in a single classroom and are "pulled out" of that classroom for ESL.

[2] Students rotate from one class to another; the ESL class is one of many regularly scheduled classes at a particular time.

[3] The focus is on fast acquisition of language skills, whether in a pull-out, departmentalized, or self-contained class.

[4] ESOL students are taught English through or in conjunction with another subject, such as science or social studies.

[5] The ESL teacher goes into a mainstream class to work with students; activities may be separately or jointly planned and conducted.

[6] The ESL teacher and content or grade-level teacher are both responsible for the class.

[7] ESOL students are placed in a grade-level classroom with both native and nonnative speakers.

Teaching and Learning Strategies	Pre-K–2						3–5						6–8						9–12					
	1	2	3	4	5	6	1	2	3	4	5	6	1	2	3	4	5	6	1	2	3	4	5	6
Computer Skills		X					X				X	X	X	X		X	X		X			X		X
Cooperative Learning				X	X					X	X				X	X			X		X			X
Critical Thinking				X						X						X				X				X
Independent Research			X				X					X	X			X	X		X					X
Literature	X	X	X	X		X	X				X									X		X		
Learning Styles	X	X		X	X				X				X	X										
Parent Involvement	X		X		X			X																
Scientific Method				X											X						X			
Use of L1							X		X		X	X	X			X	X		X				X	X

Themes and Topics	Pre-K–2						3–5						6–8						9–12					
	1	2	3	4	5	6	1	2	3	4	5	6	1	2	3	4	5	6	1	2	3	4	5	6
Animals				X																				
Building Community								X																X
Careers		X	X																					
Colonial Life								X								X								
Communities, Helpers	X		X			X	X		.	X						X								
Environment												X					X							
Exploration														X										
Family	X		X					X															X	
Games										X														
Geography								X		X			X						X					
History									X	X			X			X			X					X
Measurement															X						X			
Multiculturalism			X		X	X	X	X		X	X								X					
Native Americans				X			X																	
Nutrition		X																						
Religions, Values																	X		X					
Self	X			X				X		X													X	
Socialization	X	X								X														
Writing Genres								X								X	X						X	X

Also Available From TESOL

American Quilt: A Reference Book on American Culture
Irina Zhukova and Maria Lebedko

Common Threads of Practice:
Teaching English to Children Around the World
Katharine Davies Samway and Denise McKeon, Editors

ESL Standards for Pre-K–12 Students
TESOL

Implementing the ESL Standards for Pre-K–12 Students
Through Teacher Education
Marguerite Ann Snow, Editor

New Ways in Teaching English at the Secondary Level
Deborah J. Short, Editor

New Ways in Teaching Young Children
Linda Schinke-Llano and Rebecca Rauff, Editors

New Ways in Using Authentic Materials in the Classroom
Ruth E. Larimer and Leigh Schleicher, Editors

New Ways in Using Communicative Games in Language Teaching
Nikhat Shameem and Makhan Tickoo, Editors

New Ways of Classroom Assessment
James Dean Brown, Editor

Reading and Writing in More Than One Language:
Lessons for Teachers
Elizabeth Franklin, Editor

Teacher Education
Karen E. Johnson, Editor

Teaching in Action: Case Studies From Second Language Classrooms
Jack C. Richards, Editor

Training Others to Use the ESL Standards:
A Professional Developmental Manual
Deborah J. Short, Emily L. Gómez, Nancy Cloud, Anne Katz,
Margo Gottlieb, Margaret Malone

For more information, contact
Teachers of English to Speakers of Other Languages, Inc.
700 South Washington Street, Suite 200
Alexandria, Virginia 22314 USA
Tel 703-836-0774 • Fax 703-836-6447 • publications@tesol.org • http://www.tesol.org/